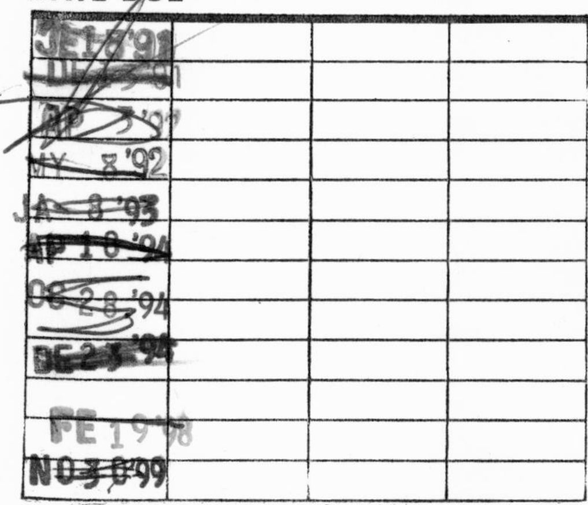

MALCOLM X

A Selected Bibliography

Compiled by
Lenwood G. Davis
With the assistance of Marsha L. Moore

Foreword by Bonnie J. Gillespie

Greenwood Press
Westport, Connecticut • London, England

Library of Congress Cataloging in Publication Data

Davis, Lenwood G.
Malcolm X, a selected bibliography.

Includes index.
1. X, Malcolm, 1925-1965—Bibliography. I. Moore, Marsha L. II. Title.
Z8989.7.D38 1983 016.297'87'0924 83-18329
[BP395.X17]
ISBN 0-313-23061-7 (lib. bdg.)

Library of Congress Catalog Card Number: 83-18329
ISBN: 0-313-23061-7

First published in 1984

Greenwood Press
A division of Congressional Information Service, Inc.
88 Post Road West, Westport, Connecticut 06881

Printed in the United States of America

10 9 8 7 6 5 4 3 2 1

Contents

Foreword

Having completed several other books and book-length bibliographies on such topics as Dr. Martin Luther King, Jr., Black Women, the Black Family, Sickle Cell Anemia, Black Artists, Marcus Garvey, the Black Elderly, Black Athletes, and Paul Robeson, Dr. Lenwood G. Davis is well qualified to write on the topic of this book, Malcolm X. His biography on Martin Luther King, Jr., in 1969, was among the first to chronicle the contributions of this great intellectual and pragmatic leader.

It has been said that if Dr. Martin Luther King, Jr., was the saint in the Black struggle or the modern revolution for Black liberation in America, then Malcolm X was the prince of the same movement. Born Malcolm Little in a small Midwest town, he later moved with his family to Detroit where he soon picked up the tricks of the trade in surviving on the streets of a large urban Black ghetto.

Through Malcolm's youth he travelled back and forth between Detroit and New York's Harlem, where he was gingerly known as Detroit Red. He had acquired this name among his fellow pimps, prostitutes, hustlers, and racketeers. Malcolm quickly earned his spurs and gained respect on the streets of the largest Black community in the United States.

After having a modicum of success as a hustler, drug pusher, and pimp in Harlem, Malcolm was arrested by the authorities and subsequently sent to an upstate New York prison, where he recorded in his autobiography that this was the freest period of his life. In the prison library he found a source of comfort and intellectual challenge in books, books, and more books. He soon became a history buff and realized that his public school education had been extremely limited and had prepared him for the failure which found him in prison. It was in prison that Malcolm began to examine his life and the condition of Blacks and other have-nots in America and around the world. He later became a Black Muslim and changed his last name to "X," to indicate that his surname "Little" was actually that of his family's former slave master. Malcolm, as a result of his leadership skills and speaking ability, became the foremost exponent and mouthpiece for the Honorable Elijah Muhammad—the leader and founder of America's Black Muslims at that time.

Malcolm had been born into an America that was stressful and at odds with itself. It was a setting where color and race where critical issues and conditions were just as W.E.B. DuBois had predicted at the turn of the twentieth century. Malcolm had been born and grew up during the tumultuous and revolutionary middle third of this twentieth century, when America was experiencing some of the following occurrences:

The Black man was "the last hired and the first fired."

Several national governmental studies on the race question had occurred (that is, *The American Dilemma, The Truman Report*, and *The Kerner Report* or *Commission*), which apparently had been shelved. Little subsequent public policy appeared to have been changed.

The inner city urban areas soon were teeming with a multitude of Blacks, minorities, various underclasses, and other general have-nots.

Black unemployment rates among adult workers were usually double those of the national average, and Black teenagers experienced rates that were often two, three, four, or even five times greater than the national unemployment rate.

Several legal decisions had been passed into law such as: (1) Truman's executive order which desegregated the U.S. Armed Forces; (2) the 1954 Supreme Court Decision which outlawed the Separate but Equal Law (*Plessy* vs. *Ferguson*) in *Brown* vs. *the Board of Education of Topeka, Kansas;* and (3) several Civil Rights and Voter Registration Laws of the early and middle 1960s were passed. All of these were enacted in an effort to insure equality, justice, and equity under the law regarding educational, occupational, and political rights for Black citizens of this country.

Blacks were generally attempting to acquire redress in nonviolent, passive resistant, and other similar ways.

An impending and onrushing involvement in the Vietnam War was increasing.

The Black community was inclined to follow and listen to the Black leader or Black would-be leader who was gifted with oratorical eloquence, persuasiveness, and charisma.

The prison population was primarily made up of have-nots (that is, poor, Blacks, and minorities), and the possession of money and class status often were strategic in the dispensation of criminal justice.

The Black community was being tempted from all sides by several competing ideologies (that is, Black Nationalism, Separatism, Cultural Nationalism, and Integrationism).

Malcolm, like several others before him such as Rev. Richard Allen, Rev. Adam Clayton Powell, and Rev. Martin Luther King, took up the mantle of the cloth by which to relate to "his people," and the Black community listened intently to what Malcolm had to say.

As a revolutionary in intellect and deed, Malcolm caught the imagination and admiration of the masses of Blacks in America. And why shouldn't he? He related well to the Black masses. He was extremely street-wise. He had a prison record. He was a preacher. And most important, he was an eloquent, fiery, and articulate speaker. But in the eyes of the Honorable Elijah Muhammad, Malcolm went too far when he made his now famous evaluation of the assassination of America's most youthful President—John F. Kennedy. Malcolm said that "the chickens had come home to roost." And that statement caused him to be silenced by Elijah Muhammad. It was not until Malcolm dropped out of the Black Muslims that he again acquired the ears of Black America. This time, however, it was under his own auspices—a new religious following of his own that was also Black Muslim.

Shortly afterwards, Malcolm went to Mecca and made the world-famous pilgrimage which broadened his philosophy and strategy of Black liberation. He no longer viewed the White man as the "blue-eyed devil," as he had when under Elijah Muhammad's tutelage. He had witnessed the multicultural, multinational, and multiracial religion of Islam in action in Mecca. And Malcolm now tended to take a more universal or international slant in his rhetoric.

It will be left up to the historians like Professor Davis to determine just what changes Malcolm made in his public pronouncements as well as his private thoughts, because shortly thereafter he also was assassinated—ironically, by other Blacks who were assumed to have been an appointed death squad of a faction of the Black Muslims. Exactly who made the decision to assassinate Malcolm still is not clear. This and other issues about Malcolm add to the swirl of controversies that surround Malcolm even in death.

Malcolm was without a doubt one of America's most dynamic and charismatic leaders to come along in quite a while. He challenged the very "foundations of the White racist society" in America, unlike any other man during his lifetime. He was among the first—if not the first—to redefine the "Movement." He advocated and perceived the Black struggle in America as a "Human Rights Movement." For Malcolm, civil rights was a parochial or national phenomenon, whereas human rights was a multinational or universal phenomenon of Blacks and have-nots internationally. Malcolm's courage, his eloquence, his self-education, his "downhomeness," and his use of the vernacular language of the streets was unparalleled within the annals of the Black American community. Malcolm was the incarnate of self-pride. His personal and positive self-affirmation presaged the later notion of "Black is Beautiful" and commensurately continued the long legacy of Negritude. Not since Marcus Garvey had a Black leader had such a Black mass appeal, admiration, and inspiration as did Malcolm X.

Dr. Davis in this single volume has captured a vast bulk of literature which will further delineate the various and multifaceted dimensions of Malcolm X's controversial and charismatic leadership. This volume has a fairly comprehensive collection of citations on books, pamphlets, speeches, articles, poetry, and phonograph records by Malcolm X. Such materials are invaluable sources for the serious scholars and researchers of Malcolm X and/or related topics.

America's media portrayed Malcolm X as a firebrand and Black radical leader who was an adamant exponent of violence. Malcolm did, in fact, often use the phrase that Blacks should acquire their freedom "by any means necessary." And violence, he felt, was one of the various tactics that Blacks had in their arsenals, if needed. He also preached that violence should be used only in "self-defense" or to protect oneself and/or family. This bibliography also shows a more gentle and rarely seen side of Malcolm through his poetry and his recorded speeches found on longplaying (33⅓) phonograph records.

Dr. Davis has put together an indispensable work and bibliographical source volume on Malcolm X—one of the most important Black leaders and revolutionaries in the twentieth century. This volume will serve well in the further scholarship and enlightenment of the intellectual and pragmatic legacy left by the late prince of the modern Black struggle—Malcolm X.

Bonnie J. Gillespie, Ph.D.
Assistant to the Director for Research
Institute for the Study of Educational Policy
Howard University

Introduction

Although much has been written about him, this is the first book-length bibliography on Malcolm X. There is a great deal of interest in his life because he was such a controversial leader. He was known not only in the United States, but also in Third World and European countries, though, ironically, he became better known after his death than when he was living. His autobiography has been translated into several foreign languages.

Although he was popular among young Blacks in the United States, he was not popular with most middle-class Blacks. Many older Blacks believe he did more than any leader to bring about division between the races, suggesting that he preached hatred of the White man by Blacks. Others believe he promoted violence and retaliation among Black people. While some of those allegations are true, most people argue that he was a man of honesty, integrity, and inpeccable character, standing up for what he believed to be right. Malcolm X not only criticized Whites, but Blacks as well, especially Black leaders such as Martin Luther King, Jr. He believed that King's nonviolent approach to racial problems was lunacy and that Black people had to fight violence with violence.

It should be pointed out that Malcolm X changed his outlook on America and its people after he visited Mecca in 1965. As he was assassinated before he could put his philosophy into action, we can only speculate on how effective he might have been if he had lived. Many people agree, however, that his new outlook and approach to problems affecting Black people would have been successful. His new philosophy had a political and economic base that appealed to all segments of the Black community. In his last year, Malcolm X appealed to other young Black leaders for support. It has been pointed out repeatedly that although Malcolm X died, his dream did not, and he inspired other young Black leaders and organizations as well. Every year since his death, celebration and commemoration services have been given in his honor. Colleges, universities, schools, streets, clubs, organizations, days, festivals, and scholarship funds have been named in his honor. Even today, Malcolm X's name sparks debate.

This bibliography deals with works by and about Malcolm X. Chapter 1 includes a book, pamphlets, manuscripts, and articles by Malcolm X. Although he wrote only one book, his autobiography, this detailed work has been hailed as a classic among autobiographical and literary works.

Chapter 2 entails major books and pamphlets about Malcolm X, many of which are biographies of the leader. Several of these were written for juveniles and young people.

Chapter 3 includes general books about Malcolm X, some of which praise him and others that bitterly criticize him. He was seen by some as a saviour and by others as a sinner. Some called him "The Ideological Father of the Black Power Movement." One writer best summed him up, perhaps, when he declared: "The key to Malcolm's rise was his grass roots origin, fiery style, and mass appeal." Some commentators on the life of Malcolm X agreed that his great contribution was "telling it like it is" in a style and manner that made America listen to the voice of an outraged man.

Chapter 4 deals with major articles about Malcolm X. Although most of these articles came from major newspapers such as the *New York Times*, and the *Washington Post*, many others came from Black newspapers such as the *New York Amsterdam News* and *The Black Panther*. The *New York Times* and the *Militant*, however, carried the most detailed reports on Malcolm X.

Also included in this chapter are many magazine, quarterly, journal, and anthology articles. It should be pointed out that several "major" articles were omitted because they could not be located.

Chapter 5 includes general articles and makes up the largest part of this book. In some instances only references to the articles were seen and not the articles themselves. These have been included without annotations because I wanted users to know that such articles were written. In other cases, when only the clipping of the article was seen and not the complete work, page numbers were not included.

The bibliography contains eight appendixes. Appendix A lists dissertations and theses; Appendix B depicts obituaries, memorials, tributes, and honors; Appendix C sites seventy-eight poems inspired by Malcolm X; Appendix D deals with reviews of a book by Malcolm and seven about him; Appendix E lists audiovisual material such as tape cassettes, most of which are part of the Schomburg Center Oral History Tape Collection; Appendix F includes records made of Malcolm X's speeches; Appendix G lists Malcolm X's namesakes, screenplay, and broadside; and Appendix H, depicts documentaries and a filmstrip about the leader. An index listing authors, joint authors, and editors rounds out this reference guide.

Any work of this nature includes the assistance of many people, and I especially would like to acknowledge a few who gave invaluable advice and assistance. Ernest Kaiser, of the Schomburg Center for Research in Black Culture, was most helpful in sharing with me a number of citations from his personal collection on the leader. Janet L. Sims-Wood, of Howard University's Moorland-Spingarn Research Center, shared with me some of the references that I was missing. I would also like to thank Kitsy Smith for typing the final copy of this work and making many corrections. I am also indebted to several libraries that assisted me: The Schomburg Center for Research in Black Culture; The Moorland-Spingarn Research Center; the Library of Congress; New York Public Library; Wake Forest University Library; the University of North Carolina at Chapel Hill Library; Duke University Library; Montclair State College; and Winston-Salem State University Library.

Although many people assisted me in this endeavor, I take full responsibility for any errors or omissions and for all of its shortcomings. As it is a *selected* bibliography, it is my hope that others will build on it, and perhaps one day we will have a *comprehensive* bibliography on Malcolm X.

MALCOLM X

1.
Works By Malcolm X

1. BOOKS, PAMPHLETS, AND MANUSCRIPT

1. Malcolm X. Talk By Malcolm X to the Class in Advanced Newswriting of the School of Journalism at Columbia University, November 20, 1963. n.p., 1963. Typewritten Manuscript Located at Columbia University.

2. Malcolm X. Malcolm X Speaks: Selected Speeches and Statements. Edited with Prefatory Notes by George Breitman. NY: Merit Publishers, 1965. 226 pp.

3. Malcolm X. Malcolm X Talks to Young People. NY: The Young Socialist, 1965 (Pamphlet).

4. Malcolm X. Two Speeches by Malcolm X. NY: Pioneer Publishers, 1965. 31 pp.

5. Malcolm X. Two Speeches by Malcolm X. NY: Pathfinder Press, 1970. 31 pp.

6. Malcolm X. The Autobiography of Malcolm X (With the Assistance of Alex Haley), NY: Grove Press, 1965. 460 pp.

7. Malcolm X. Der Schwarze Tribrun; Malcolm X, Eine Autobiographie. Hrsg. von Alex Haley. Mit Einem Vorwort Kon Klaus Harpprecht. Aus Dem Amerikanischen Von G. Danehl. Frankfurt am Main: S. Fischer, 1966. 411 pp.

8. Malcolm X. L'Autobiographie de Malcolm X. Avec la collaboration de Alex Haley. Tradint par Anne Guerin. Introduction de Daniel Guerin. Paris: B. Grasset, 1966. 331 pp.

9. Malcolm X. Autobiografia di Malcolm. Redatta con la collaborazione di Alex Haley. Introduzione, traduzione e note di Roberto Giammanco, Torino, G. Einaudi, 1967. 453 pp.

10. Malcolm X. The Speeches of Malcolm X at Harvard. Edited with an Introductory Essay by Archie Epps. NY: William Morrow, 1968. 191 pp.

11. Malcolm X. Malcolm X and The Negro Revolution: The Speeches of Malcolm X. Edited with an Introductory Essay by Archie Epps. London: Owen, 1969. 192 pp.

12. Malcolm X. By Any Means Necessary: Speeches, Interviews, and a Letter, by Malcolm X. Edited by George Breitman. NY: Pathfinder Press, 1970. 184 pp.

13. Malcolm X. Malcolm X On Afro-American History. Expanded and Illustrated Edition. NY: Merit Book, 1970. 74 pp.

14. Malcolm X. The End of White World Supremacy: Four Speeches. Edited and with an Introduction by Benjamin Goodman. The four speeches in this Collection are: "Black Man's History," "The Black Revolution," "The Old Negro and the New Negro," and "God's Judgment of White America." (The Chickens Are Coming Home To Roost.)

II. ARTICLES

A Selected List

15. Malcolm X. "Angry Spokesman Malcolm X Tells Off Whites," Life. Vol. 54, No. 22, May 31, 1963, pp. 30-31.

16. Malcolm X. "Black Revolution," The Militant, April 27, 1964, pp. 5-6. This is the text of a speech that Malcolm X delivered to the Militant Labor Forum at New York's Palm Gardens Ballroom on April 8th.

17. Malcolm X. "Malcolm X's Letters to US (From the Near East and Africa) Describe Welcome in Africa," The Militant, May 25, 1964, p. 6. Malcolm X declares in the letter: "Despite Western propaganda to the contrary, our African Brothers and Sisters love us, and are happy to learn that we also are awakening from our long 'sleep' and are developing strong love for them."

18. Malcolm X. "We Are all Blood Brothers," Liberator, July, 1964, pp. 4-6.

19. Malcolm X. "Racism: The Cancer That Is Destroying America," Egyptian Gazette, August 25, 1964.

20. Malcolm X. "I'm Talking to You, White Man; Excerpt from Autobiography of Malcolm X, by Alex Haley and Malcolm X." Saturday Evening Post, Vol. 237, No. 31, September 12, 1964, pp. 30-32.

21. Malcolm X. "Power in Defense of Freedom Is Greater Than Power in Behalf of Tyranny," The Militant, January 25, 1965, p. 5. This is an excerpt from a speech delivered by Malcolm X at the Militant Labor Forum in New York on January 7th.

22. Malcolm X Speaks, The Militant, October 25, 1965, Installment 1, p. 4; November 1, 1965, Installment 2, p. 4; November 8, 1965, Installment 3, p. 4; November 15, 1965, Installment 4, p. 4; November 22, 1965, Installment 5, p. 4; November 29, 1965, Installment 6, p. 4; December 6, 1965, Installment 7, p. 4; December 13, 1965, Installment 8, p. 4; December 20, 1965, Installment 9, p. 4; December 27, 1965, Installment 10, p. 4; January 3, 1966, Installment 12, p. 4; January 17, 1966, Installment 13, p. 4; January 24, 1966, Installment 14, p. 4; February 7, 1966, Installment 15, p. 4; February 14, 1966, Installment 16, p. 4; March 7, 1966, Installment 18, p. 4; March 14, 1966, Installment 19, p. 4; March 21, 1966, Installment 20, p. 4; March 28, 1966, Installment 21, p. 2; April 4, 1966, Installment 22, p. 2; April 11, 1966, Installment 23, p. 2; April 18, 1966, Installment 24, p. 2; April 25, 1966, Installment 25, p. 2; May 9, 1966, Installment 26, p. 2.

23. Malcolm X. "The Black Struggle in the United States," Presence Africaine (English Edition), 2nd Quarter, 1965, pp. 8-24.

24. Malcolm X. "Afro-American History," International Socialist Review, Vol. 28, No. 2, March-April 1967, pp. 3-48. Whole issue devoted to this article. Introduction to article by George Breitman.

25. Malcolm X. "God's Judgment of White America," (Speech) Evergreen Review, Vol. 50, December 1967, pp. 54-60.

26. Malcolm X. "Letters From Mecca and Other Comments," The Black Power Revolt, Floyd B. Barbour, Editor. Boston: Porter-Sargent Publisher, 1968, pp. 7, 8, 89, 102, 105, 129, 136-138, 185, 186, 227, 229, 230, 231, 233, 240-244.

27. Malcolm X. "The Last Message," The Black Panther, February 28, 1970, p. 16.

28. Malcolm X. "Malcolm X Talks to Young People," The Black Panther, May 19, 1970, pp. 12-13.

2.
Major Books and Pamphlets About Malcolm X

A Selected List

29. Adoff, Arnold. Malcolm X, NY: Thomas Y. Crowell Co., 1970. 41 pp. Written for juveniles.

30. Baldwin, James. One Day, When I Was Lost: A Scenario Based on Alex Haley's The Autobiography of Malcolm X, London: Michael Joseph, 1972. 167 pp.

31. Boesak, Allan. Coming Out of the Wilderness: A Comparative Interpretation of the Ethnic of Martin Luther King, Jr. and Malcolm X. Kampen, Holland: J. H. Kok, 1976. 48 pp.

32. Breitman, George. Malcolm X: The Man and His Ideas, NY: Pioneer Publishers, March 1965. (Pamphlet). 22 pp.

33. ________________. The Last Year of Malcolm X: The Evolution of a Revolutionary. NY: Merit Publishing, 1966. 169 pp.

34. ________________, Herman Porter, and Baxter Smyth. The Assassination of Malcolm X. NY: Pathfinder Press, 1976. 190 pp.

35. Clarke, John Henrik. Malcolm X: The Man and His Times. NY: Macmillan, 1969. 360 pp.

36. Cleage, Albert B. Myths About Malcolm X: Two Views By Rev. Albert Cleage and George Breitman. NY: Merit Publishers, 1968. 30 pp.

37. Curtis, Richard. The Life of Malcolm X. Philadelphia: Macrae Smith Co., 1971. 160 pp.

38. Goldman, Peter Louis. The Death and Life of Malcolm X. NY: Harper & Row, 1973. 438 pp.

39. Goodman, Benjamin, Editor. The End of White World Supremacy: Four Speeches of Malcolm X. NY: Merlin House, Inc., 1971. 148 pp. The four speeches are: "Black Man's History," "The Black Revolution," "The Old Negro and the New Negro," and "God's Judgment of White America."

40. Haskins, James. The Picture Life of Malcolm X. NY: Frank Watts, 1975. 43 pp. Written for Kindergarten to Grade 3.

41. Jamal, Hakim Abdullah. (Formerly Allen Donaldson) From The Dead Level: Malcolm X And Me. NY: Random House, 1972. 240 pp.

42. Lomax, Louis E. When the Word Is Given: A Report on Elijah Muhammad, Malcolm X, and Black Muslim World. Cleveland: World Publishing Co., 1963. 192 pp.

43. Maglangbayan, Shawna. Garvey, Lumumba and Malcolm: Black National-Separatists. Chicago: Third World Press, 1972. (Malcolm X. pp. 69-108, 111-117.)

44. Malcolm X Memorial Committee. Brother Malcolm. NY: Malcolm X Memorial Committee, 1965. 23 pp. Cover title, "Excerpts From Brave Shepherd of Black Sheep" by Sara Mitchell.

45. Moore, William Henry. On Identity and Consciousness of El Hajj Malik El Shabazz (Malcolm X). Santa Cruz, CA: n.p., 1974.

46. Nagata, Ei. The Black Revolt: Malcolm X, The Man and His Ideas. Tokyo: Sanichi Shobo, 1966.

47. Nordon, Eric. The Murder of Malcolm X. NY: Realist, 1966. (Pamphlet.)

48. Randall, Dudley and Margaret G. Burroughs, Editors. For Malcolm: Poems on the Life and Death of Malcolm X. Detroit: Broadside Press, 1969. 127 pp.

49. White, Florence Maiman. Malcolm X: Black and Proud. Champaign, IL: Garrard Publishing Co., 1975. 95 pp. Written for juveniles.

50. Wolfenstein, Eugene V. The Victims of Democracy: Malcolm X and The Black Revolution. Los Angeles: University of California Press, 1981. 432 pp.

3.

General Books About Malcolm X

A Selected List

51. Adams, A. John and Joan Martin Burke. Civil Rights: A Current Guide To The People, Organizations and Events. NY: R. R. Bowker Co., 1970. Malcolm X. pp. 12, 18, 27, 31, 34, 60, 62, 64, 74, 80, 90, 106, 148.

    Authors discuss Malcolm X and his relationships with the Nation of Islam and the Organization of Afro-American Unity. Malcolm X founded the latter organization.

52. Adams, Russel L. Great Negro: Past and Present. Chicago: Afro-American Publishing Co., 1976. Third Edition. "Malcolm X: Martyred Militant," p. 131.

    The writer concludes: "Most commentators on the life of Malcolm X agreed that his great contribution was 'telling it like it is' in a style and manner that made America listen to the voice of an outraged man".

53. Afro-American Encyclopedia. North Miami, FL: Educaational Book Publishers, Inc., 1974. Vol. 6. Malcolm X, pp. 1563-1567.

    A short biographical sketch of Malcolm X is included in this collection.

54. Alexander, Rae Pace and Julius Lester. Young and Black in America. NY: Random House, 1970. Malcolm X, pp. 57-68.

    Writers conclude: "Today Malcolm X stands as one of the Black Saints in history not only in the United States, but wherever Blacks gather in the name of Liberation".

55. Allen, Gary. Communist Revolution in the Streets. Boston: Western Islands, 1967. Malcolm X, pp. 1, 3, 6, 7, 8, 9, 10, 12, 18, 19, 43, 52.

Author concludes that Malcolm X was the Lenin of the Black Revolution.

56. Allen, Robert L. Black Awakening in Capitalist America: An Analytic History. Garden City, NY: Doubleday & Co., Inc., 1969. Malcolm X, pp. 5, 20, 26-34, 40, 41, 94, 95, 96, 115, 207, 208; assassinated, 26, 34.

Author declares that Malcolm was the Ideological Father of the Black Power Movement and one man who Harlem's angry masses looked to for new leadership.

57. _______________. A Guide to Black Power in America: A Historical Analysis. London: Victor Gollancz, Ltd., 1970. Malcolm X, pp. 5, 20, 26-34, 40, 41, 94, 95, 96, 115, 207, 208; assassinated, 26, 34.

The author mentions that Malcolm X was the Ideological Father of The Black Power Movement.

58. Anderson, Jervis. A. Philip Randolph: A Biographical Portrait. NY: Hacourt, Brace, Jovanovich, 1972. Malcolm X, pp. 13, 14, 321.

The writer asserts Malcolm X once declared: "All civil rights leaders are confused, but Randolph is less confused than the rest." Randolph was the only one of the major civil rights leaders who invited Malcolm to meetings of common interest to Blacks in New York.

59. Anthony, Earl. Picking up the Gun: A Report on the Black Panthers. NY: Dial Press, 1970. Malcolm X, pp. 3, 4, 6, 11, 17, 48, 49, 67, 101, 103, 112.

The writer discusses the week long commemoration of the death of Malcolm X in San Francisco-Oakland, in February, 1967. He surmises that the White Lefts always pit Black personalities against each other, ideologically, and the mass media uses any differences between personalities to create a situation of drama and melodrama for the public. Anthony concludes: "I firmly believe that this is what set the stage for Malcolm X to be assassinated!"

60. Aya, Roderick and Norman Miller, Editors. The New American Revolution. NY: Free Press, 1971. Malcolm X, pp. 115, 117, 175-180, 183-184, 209, 212.

The editors surmised that Malcolm X's radicalism was in the mold of Tom Paine, John Adams, and John Brown. It was also suggested that the key to Malcolm's rise was his grass-roots origin, fiery style, and mass appeal.

61. Baldwin, James. No Name in the Street. NY: The Dial Press, 1972. Malcolm X, pp. 11, 78, 91, 92, 93, 94, 95, 96, 97, 98, 99, 132.

The writer mentions how he first met Malcolm X.

62. ______________. The Fire Next Time. NY: The Dial Press, 1963. Malcolm X, pp. 73, 74, 96.

The author discusses how he met Malcolm. He also states that Malcolm was the Black Muslims "Movement's second-in-command, and heir apparent."

63. Banks, William L. The Black Church in the U.S.: It's Origin, Growth, Contributions, and Outlook. Chicago, IL: University of Chicago Press, 1972. Malcolm X, pp. 67-69.

This is a brief discussion of Malcolm X's rise and fall in The Nation of Islam.

64. Baraka, Imamu Amiri (LeRoi Jones). Raise, Race, Rays, Raze: Essays Since 1965. NY: Random House, 1971. Malcolm X, pp. 29, 30, 31, 32, 128, 145, 146.

The author concludes that the concept of Black Power is natural after Malcolm X. He suggests that Malcolm's legacy was the concept and will toward political power in the world for the Black Man.

65. Barbour, Floyd. The Black Power Revolt: A Collection of Essays. Boston, MA: Extending Horizons Books, 1968. Malcolm X, pp. 137, 138, 164, 185, 186, 227, 230, 231, 240, 241, 242, 243, 244.

Malcolm X's Letters from Mecca are included in this work.

66. ______________. The Black Seventies. Boston, MA: Porter Sargent Publisher, 1970. Malcolm X, pp. 10, 16, 19, 187.

The author declares that Malcolm X definitely learned his nationalism from the Black Muslims, who provided him with the means of expressing the latent beliefs of all Black People.

67. Barker, Lucius J. and Jesse J. McCorry, Jr. Black Americans and the Political System. Cambridge, MA: Winthrop Publishers, Inc., 1976. Malcolm X, p. 220.

The writers state that the Black Muslims gained national attention during the early 1960's, under the leadership of Elijah Muhammad and Malcolm X, as an alternative to racial integration.

68. Bedell, George C., et. al. Religion in America. NY: Macmillan Co., 1975. Malcolm X, pp. 350-362.

    There is a biographical study of Malcolm X in this work.

69. Bell, Inge Powell. CORE and The Strategy of Nonviolence. NY: Random House, 1968. Malcolm X, pp. 49-50, 176-177.

    The author concludes that more significant than the new organization, (Organization for Afro-American Unity) that he founded was the philosophy that he brought to the political action program further in the direction of political independence begun by Malcolm X and others.

70. Bennett, Lerone, Jr. Before the Mayflower: A History of Black America. Chicago, IL: Johnson Publishing Co., 1969. pp. 356, 358.

    Mr. Bennett points out that Malcolm X called for a socioeconomic program of self-defense and self-assertion in concert with the emerging nations of Africa. Malcolm X's assassination and the turbulent upheaval that followed refocused attention on the restless ghetto and lent new urgency to the Negro's quest for new instruments of liberation, states the author.

71. _____. Confrontation: Black and White. Chicago, IL: Johnson Publishing Co., 1965. Malcolm X, pp. 205-207, 211-213, 216, 276, 278, 290, 294.

    The writer suggests: "Malcolm X in sum, prepared the way for Martin Luther King's rebellion. Only time will tell if King, in turn, prepared the way of Malcolm X's succession."

72. Bergman, Peter M. The Chronological History of the Negro in America. NY: Harper & Row, 1969. Malcolm X, pp. 419, 593.

    The writer mentions Malcolm X's birth and death.

73. Bernardo, Stephanie. The Ethnic Almanac. Garden City, NY: Dolphin Books, 1981. Malcolm X, pp. 15, 171.

    Author discusses Malcolm's name change from Malcolm Little, to Malcolm X, to El Hajj Malik El Shabazz.

74. Berry, Mary Frances. Black Resistance White Law: A History of Constitutional Racism in America. NY: Meredith Corp., 1971. Malcolm X, pp. 210, 211.

    It was pointed out that in 1959 Malcolm X, the articulate spokesman for Elijah Muhammad's Black Muslims, gained national attention for his analysis of the shallowness of earlier civil movements and their leadership and his program for Black Nationalism.

75. ________________ and John W. Blassingame. Long Memory: The Black Experience in America. NY: Oxford University Press, 1982. Malcolm X, pp. 102, 111, 183, 184, 244, 333, 359, 385, 386, 393, 417, 421, 422.

The writers argue that in the face of all the beatings and bombings, Malcolm X's voice seemed to be one of reason, while that of Martin Luther King, Jr., James Farmer of CORE, and Whitney Young of the Urban League, appeared to be utopian. Youthful Blacks were especially attracted by the proud defiance, sharp mind, and vision of manhood that Malcolm projected.

76. Berton, Pierre, Editor. Voices From the Sixties. Garden City, NY: Doubleday & Co., 1967. See "Malcolm X: The Black Vigilante," pp. 31-41.

This was Malcolm X's last television appearance with the editor in Toronto, Canada on January 19, 1965. About a month later he was assassinated in New York City.

77. Blair, Thomas L. Retreat to the Ghetto: The End of a Dream? NY: Hill and Wang, 1977. Malcolm X, pp. vii, viii, xvii-xx, 25, 28-60, 69-70, 72-75, 81, 86-89, 91, 93, 95-96, 100, 104, 112, 115, 118, 120, 132, 142, 154, 156, 192, 194, 206. Chapter Two, pp. 28-60 is entitled "Separatism: The Legacy of Malcolm X."

The author argues that during Malcolm X's life, no Black leader was free from the shadow of his thinking; in fact, he was singularly responsible for the demystification of the Civil Rights Movement and was precursor of the rise of Black Power.

78. Boggs, James. Racism and the Class Struggle: Further Pages From a Black Worker's Notebook. NY: Monthly Review Press, 1970. Malcolm X, pp. 44, 51, 52, 110, 111, 112, 113, 114, 115, 116, 124.

The author concludes that Malcolm's political life, though brief, left an ineradicable impact on the Black Movement and the Black masses, because he led the movement from the civil rights stage to the stage of struggle for Black Power.

79. Bond, Julian. A Time to Speak, a Time to Act: The Movement in Politics. NY: Simon and Schuster, 1972. Malcolm X, p. 145.

The author states that we cannot afford to mouth the admirable rhetoric of Malcolm X without also adopting his admirable self-discipline.

80. Bontemps, Arna and Jack Conroy. Anyplace But Here. NY: Hill and Wang, 1945. Malcolm X (Malcolm Little), pp. 230-244.

This work discusses Malcolm X's relationship with the Black Muslims.

81. Bosmajian, Haig A. and Hamida Bosmajian, Compilers. The Rhetoric of the Civil Rights Movement. NY: Random House, 1969.

A debate at Cornell University by Malcolm X and James Farmer is included in this collection.

82. Bracey, John H., Jr. et al, Editors. Black Nationalism in America. Indianapolis: Bobbs-Merrill Co., Inc., 1970. Malcolm X, pp. viii, xlviii, 412-427, 449-451, 504-505.

"Minister Malcolm X Enunciates the Muslim Program," "The Organization of Afro-American Unity for Human Rights and Dignity," are discussed.

83. Brink, William and Louis Harris. Revolution in America. NY: Simon and Schuster, 1963. Malcolm X, pp. 49, 118, 136, 245.

The authors state that whatever one might think of the Black Muslims, their New York leader, Malcolm X, had a point when he told Newsweek that no White could possibly understand the empathy which passes between two Negroes when they exchange glances or simply say, "Man."

84. Brisbane, Robert H. Black Activism: Racial Revolution in the United States, 1954-1970. Valley Froge, PA: Judson Press, 1974. Malcolm X, pp. 62, 70, 72, 96, 105-124, 128, 139, 147, 153, 157, 172, 177, 179-180, 195-196, 201-202, 205, 224, 272, 279, 281, 283-284, 291.

Chapter 5 is entitled "Malcolm X," and discussed the assassination of the leader.

85. __________________. The Black Vanguard: Origins of the Negro Social Revolution, 1900-1960. Valley Forge, PA: Judson Press, 1970. Malcolm X, pp. 214-216.

It is stated that by the time of his death in 1965, Malcolm X had gained recognition as the Number One Black Muslim in the country.

86. Breitman, George, Harold Cruse, and Clifton DeBerry. Marxism and the Negro Struggle. NY: Pioneer Publishers, 1965. Malcolm X, p. 44.

Malcolm X indicated at a public meeting that in his African and Asian travels, he discerned that many people politics to be "socialism."

87. Brooks, Thomas R. Walls Come Tumbling Down: A History of the Civil Rights Movement, 1940-1970. Englewood Cliffs, NJ: Prentice-Hall, Inc., 1974. Malcolm X, pp. 215-216, 232, following of, 265, 1963 March on Washington, 220.

The writer surmises that Malcolm X credited President John F. Kennedy with orchestration of the 1963 March on Washington.

88. Burns, William Haywood. The Voices of Negro Protest in America. NY: Oxford University Press, 1963. Malcolm X, pp. 33, 66, 69, 75, 76-79.

The writer points out the role Malcolm X played in the Nation of Islam. It was also stated that during Fidel Castro's visit to New York City in 1960, Malcolm X was reported to have had a prolonged and closed consultation with the Cuban leader at a time when no one else was being permitted to see him.

89. Carlisle, Rodney. The Roots of Black Nationalism. Port Washington, NY: Kennikat Press, 1965. Malcolm X (Malcolm Little), pp. 145-149, 151.

The author declares that the most serious schism to develop in the ranks of the Nation of Islam came as a result of the departure of Malcolm X in 1964. Malcolm X was the best-known Muslim Minister, and the one individual, who more than any other, secularized Elijah Muhammad's doctrines, revived and spread Black Nationalist ideas, and reshaped Black American thinking in the mid-1960's.

90. Carmichael, Stokely. Stokely Speaks: Black Power Back to Pan-Africanism. NY: Random House, 1971. Malcolm X, pp. 129, 188, 189-191, 197, 198, 205, 217, 219, 223-224.

The author compares Malcolm X's role as a Leader with Martin Luther King, Jr.'s. Malcolm X is also discussed as a Pan-Africanist.

91. Carson, Calyborne. In Struggle: SNCC and The Black Awakening of the 1960s. Cambridge, MA: Harvard University Press, 1981. Malcolm X, pp. 2, 4, 100, 103, 135-136, 192, 215, 279.

The writer suggests that Malcolm's Pan-African perspective and his awareness of the need for Black self-defense and racial pride converged with the ideas gaining acceptance in SNCC.

92. Chafe, William H. Civilities and Civil Rights: Greensboro, North Carolina and the Black Struggle for Freedom. NY: Oxford University Press, 1980. Malcolm X, pp. 246, 258, 260, 274, 312, 326.

Malcolm X is discussed in this work as a major Black leader in America.

93. Chambers, Bradford, Editor. Chronicles of Black Protest. NY: Mentor Books, 1968. Malcolm X, pp. 201-202.

One section in this work is entitled: "Malcolm X and The Black Muslims: 1964." The subtitle of the article is: "Two Points of View on Black Nationalism," by Elijah Muhammad and Malcolm X.

94. Chapman, Abraham, Editor. Black Voices: An Anthology of Afro-American Literature. NY: New American Library, 1968. Malcolm X, pp. 332-347.

Chapter One: "Nightmare," of The Autobiography of Malcolm X, is included in this collection.

95. Clark, Kenneth Bancroft. The Negro Protest: James Baldwin, Malcolm X, Martin Luther King, Talk with Kenneth B. Clark. Boston: Beacon, 1963.

The title tells what this work is about.

96. Cleage, Albert B., Jr. Black Christian Nationalism: New Directions for the Black Church. NY: William Morrow & Co., Inc., 1972. Malcolm X, pp. 79, 91, 104-119, 124. Chapter 7 is entitled, "The Philosophy of Brother Malcolm."

The author states that of all the national Black Leaders, including Martin Luther King, Jr., Malcolm X was the only one who could understand the pragmatic realism of Black Christian Nationalsim as it was developed at the Shrine of the Black Madonna in Detroit, Michigan.

97. Cleaver, Eldridge. Soul on Ice. NY: McGraw-Hill, 1968. Malcolm X, pp. 50-61, 66, 209.

There is a section entitled, "Initial Reaction on the Assassination of Malcolm X." The author discusses Malcolm's appeal to Black convicts.

98. Cohen, Rabbi Henry. Justice, Justice: A Jewish View of the Black Revolution. NY: Union of American Hebrew Congregations, 1969. Malcolm X, pp. 28-29, 117-118.

It was stated that the most popular hero among self-determinists was Malcolm X, who while serving a prison sentence, was converted to the Muslim religious nationalism of Elijah Muhammad.

99. Coleman, Emmett. The Rise, Fall, and . . .? of Adam Clayton Powell. NY: Bee-Line Books, 1967. Malcolm X, p. 145.

The author states that in the summer of 1964, Malcolm X, who had recently broken with the Black Muslims, flew to Selma, Alabama to give a speech concerning political action.

100. Cone, James H. Black Theology and Black Power. NY: Seabury Press, 1969. Malcolm X, pp. 17-18, 21, 28, 40, 48. 131.

Malcolm X's views on White people, who he called "devils," are discussed.

101. ____________. Black Theology and Black Power. NY: Seabury Press, 1970. Malcolm X, pp. 17-18, 21, 28.

The author discusses Malcolm X's opinion of Whites. He states: "Theologically, Malcolm X was not far wrong when he called the White man, 'The Devil!'"

102. Cook, Mercer and Stephen E. Henderson. The Militant Black Writer in Africa and The United States. Madison: University of Wisconsin Press, 1969. Malcolm X, pp. 69-71, 84, 99, 102, 110-114, 120.

The writers conclude that in some ways, Malcolm X's death was more tragic than Martin Luther King, Jr.'s for the Civil Rights Movement had moved North and Malcolm had the potential of unifying elements in the Black community that King could not reach.

103. Coombs, Norman. The Black Experience in America. NY: Twayne Publishers, Inc., 1972. Malcolm X, pp. 169, 211-213, 216.

It was stated that Malcolm X gave the Black Muslims Movement the organizational skill and the eloquence which it previously lacked. It was also suggested that Malcolm X was able to appeal to ghetto residents in a way that Martin Luther King, Jr. could not.

104. Cox, David, et. al, Editors. How Does a Minority Group Achieve Power? A Case Study of Black Americans (1954 to the Present). NY: John Wiley & Sons, Inc., 1969. Malcolm X, pp. 66-71.

The authors declare that during the latter part of 1964, and early 1965, Malcolm X re-evaluated the method by which Black Americans could best obtain power in a White society.

105. Cruse, Harold. The Crisis of the Negro Intellectual. NY: William Morrow & Co., 1967. Malcolm X, pp. 6, 242, 273, 355, 405, 408, 409, 416, 421, 430, 441-443, 492, 548, 557-558, 563-564.

The writer argues that no matter how nationalistic Malcolm X remained after his break with the Nation of Islam, he was forced by circumstances to swing closer to the Civil Rights Integrationist forces in order to participate more fully in the broad struggle. Mr. Cruse also surmises that after Malcolm X's death, the Black Power Slogan was actually a swing back to the conservative nationalism from which Malcolm X had just departed.

106. ______________. Rebellion or Revolution? NY: William Morrow & Co., 1968. Malcolm X, pp. 73, 199, 200, 207-213.

The writer suggests that Malcolm X remained a militant Black Nationalist until the moment he died. He concludes: "He was evolving into something undefinable because present circumstances make definitions highly conjectural and tentative."

107. David, Jay and Catherine J. Greene, Editors. Black Roots: An Anthology. NY: Lothrop, Lee & Shepard Co., 1971. Malcolm X, pp. 195-210.

This was an excerpt from "Nightmare" that was reprinted from The Autobiography of Malcolm X.

108. Davis, Arthur P. and Saunders Redding, Editors. Cavalcade: Negro American Writing from 1760 to the Present. Boston, MA: Houghton Mifflin Co., 1971. Malcolm X, pp. 739-757.

"Saved" is included in this collection and was Chapter X from The Autobiography of Malcolm X.

109. Davis, Lenwood G. I Have a Dream: The Life and Times of Martin Luther King, Jr. Westport, CT: Greenwood Press, 1973. Malcolm X, pp. 69, 170, 202.

The writer states that Malcolm X warned that the patience of the American Negro was wearing thin in the fight for the equal rights. Malcolm X implied that violence was near at hand.

110. ________________. A Paul Robeson Research Guide. Westport, CT: Greenwood Press, 1982. Malcolm X, See numbers 1733, 1843, 1874, 1884, 2070, 2123, 2124.

The author states that Malcolm X was a martyr just like Paul Robeson.

111. D'Emilio, John. The Civil Rights Struggle: Leaders in Profile. NY: Facts On File, 1979. Malcolm X - Profile, pp. 97-98. See also pp. 42, 169, 179.

Malcolm X is discussed in this work.

112. De Lerma, Dominique - Rene. Reflections on Afro-American Music. Kent, OH: Kent State University Press, 1973. Malcolm X, pp. 101-102, 109, 187; and "Black America" (Baker), 96 - 97.

The author states the influence that Malcolm X had on Black music. He also surmises that "Soul" is an awareness of brotherhood - from Martin Luther King, Jr. to Malcolm . . . .

113. Dennis, R. Ethel. The Black People of America: Illustrated History. NY: McGraw-Hill Book Co., 1970. Malcolm X, pp. 355-358.

The author states that probably the most dynamic personality among the Muslims, is certainly the most featured in the White press, was Elijah Muhammed's chief minister Malcolm X. Stern, intense, self-disciplined, Malcolm demonstrated Muslims' potential for personal fulfillment concludes Dennis.

114. Doren, Charles Van, Editor. Webster's American Biographies. Springfield, MA: G & C Merriam Co., 1974. Malcolm X, pp. 683-684.

There is a short biographical sketch of Malcolm X. The editor concludes: "In the wake of his death, his often radical disagreements with other Black Leaders were largely forgotten, and he quickly achieved the status of a cultural hero for a new and activist generation of Black Americans."

115. Dormon, James H. and Robert R. Jones. The Afro-American Experience: A Cultural History Through Emancipation. NY: John Wiley & Sons, Inc., 1974. Malcolm X, p. 99.

The authors stated that Malcolm X, a most perceptive and sensitive observer of Afro-American matters, told a Black audience on one occasion, that "no matter how long you and I have been over here, we aren't American yet."

116. Draper, Theodore. The Rediscovery of Black Nationalism. NY: Viking Press, 1969. Malcolm X, pp. 86-96, 99, 101-102, 117, 133-135.

Chapter 6 is entitled, "Malcolm X." It concluded that to the extent that Malcolm X related Afro-American liberation in particular to African liberation in general, he might be said to be an exponent of a kind of international Black revolutionary emigrationism.

117. Drimmer, Melvin, Editor. Black History: A Reappraisal. Garden City, NY: Doubleday & Co., Inc., 1968. Malcolm X, pp. 388, 446, 456, 468-481, 512, 513, 522.

It was stated that one of the most remarkable autobiographical accounts in the whole of American letters was published in 1965 with the appearance of The Autobiography of Malcolm X.

118. Ducas, George, Editor. Great Documents in Black American History. NY: Praeger Publishers, 1970. LeRoi Jones, "The Legacy of Malcolm X and The Coming of The Black American History," pp. 307-313. Malcolm X, pp. 167, 231.

119. Dulles, Foster Rhea. The Civil Rights Commission: 1957-1965. East Lansing, MI: Michigan State University Press, 1968. Malcolm X, p. 219.

"Malcolm X: Unenthusiastic Over 1964 Civil Rights Act," is included in this work.

120. Dye, Thomas R. The Politics of Equality. NY: The Bobbs-Merrill Co., Inc., 1971. Malcolm X, pp. 136-141, 193 - 194.

This work states that Malcolm X has assumed greater eminence after his death than he ever enjoyed during his lifetime. He has been elevated to the status of folk hero among many militant Black youths.

121. Editors of Ebony. Ebony Pictoral History of Black America. Nashville, TN: Southwestern Co., 1971. Vol. III. Malcolm X, pp. 26, 51, 70-71, 80, 106, 156, 265, 266, 271.

This work includes: against migration to Africa, 83; assassination of, 80; and Black Nationalism, 83; and Black Power Movement, 83; Elijah Muhammad, 80, 85; fighter for Black Liberation of Afro-American Unity, 83; influence on Newton and Seale, 94-95; opposition to integration, 81-82; philosophy on coalition with Whites, 80-82; theory of self-defense, 82.

122. ________________. The Black Revolution. Chicago, IL: Johnson Publishing Co., 1970. Malcolm X, pp. 9, 32, 46, 47, 49, 57, 68, 155, 162, 172, 202, 225 - 226.

Malcolm X is discussed throughout this work in the various reprinted essays.

123. Editors of Freedomways. Paul Robeson: The Great Forerunner. NY: Dodd, Mead & Co., 1978. Malcolm X, pp. 180, 182, 186.

It was stated that young Blacks had heard of Malcolm X but had not heard of Paul Robeson.

124. Edwards, Harry. The Struggle That Must Be: An Autobiography. NY: Macmillan Publishing Co., 1980. Malcolm X, pp. 139, 146, 158, 166, 167, 168, 170, 172, 183, 269, 272, 320, 322, 332.

The author discussed the impact that Malcolm X had on his thinking and life.

125. Ellis, William W. White Ethics and Black Power: The Emergence of the West Side Organization. Chicago, IL: Aldine Publishing Co., 1969. Malcolm X, pp. xi, 63-66.

The writer declares that the leaders, thoughts, and outlook of the West Side Organization were paralled to Malcolm X.

126. Ellison, Mary. The Black Experience: American Blacks Since 1865. NY: Harper & Row Publishers, Inc., 1974. Malcolm X, pp. 240, 241-243.

It was stated that by 1965, Malcolm X had moved beyond Black nationalism as his sustaining goal had replaced it with an impulse for revolutionary change which could be promoted by Whites as well as Blacks.

127. Essien-Udom, Essien Udosen. Black Nationalism: A Search For a Black Identity in America. NY: Dell Publishing Co., 1962. Minister Malcolm X, pp. 83, 93, 94, 104, 114-116, 121, 169, 177, 186, 194, 207, 217, 243, 290, 291, 307, 321, 325, 339, 371, 376.

Malcolm X's role in the Black Muslims is discussed throughout this book.

128. ____________________ and Amy Jacques Garvey, Editors. More Philosophy and Opinions of Marcus Garvey, Selected and Edited from Previously Unpublished Material. Vol. III. London: Frank Cass, 1977.

This work was dedicated to Brother Malcolm X Shabbazz, Osaggefo Kwane Nkjumah and Edward Wilmiot Blyden.

129. Fager, Charles E. White Reflections on Black Power. Grand Rapids, MI: William B. Eerdmans Publishing Co., 1967. Malcolm X, pp. 24, 25, 48, 106.

The author discusses Malcolm X's presence in Selma, Alabama in 1965. He told the people that the White people should thank Dr. Martin Luther King, Jr. for holding people in check, for there are others who do not believe in these measures.

130. Farmer, James. Freedom---When? NY: Random House, 1966. Malcolm X, pp. 94-101.

Author concludes that Malcolm X, in part was the creature of the press and television, which have inflated more than one Black reputation with their attention. Precisely because so much of what he said was so valid psychologically, Malcolm X and his heirs have succeeded in discrediting the whole philosophy of non-violence in the eyes of many Blacks.

131. Fax, Elton C. Contemporary Black Leaders. NY: Dodd, Mead & Co., 1970. Malcolm X, pp. 1-19.

Writer points out people the world over, especially young people who believe in the dignity of all human beings, know and revere Malcolm X's name. He concludes: "Surely no greater tribute can be paid to any man."

132. Fisher, Sethard, Editor. Power and The Black Community: A Reader on Racial Subordination in the United States. NY: Random House, 1970. Malcolm X, pp. 227, 250.

Author states that Malcolm X best embodied the belief that racism was so deeply ingrained in White America that appeal to conscience would bring no fundamental change.

133. Foner, Eric, Editor. America's Black Past: A Reader in Afro-American History. NY: Harper & Row Publishers, 1970. Malcolm X, pp. 459, 460, 473, 474-477, 478, 479, 480, 540, 549, 553- 534.

Author states that first among the Black rebels to be cut down in the classic American style - by gunfire at a public meeting - Malcolm X had become a martyr and a saint even before his last breath escaped his body. Just before and just after his death a new flowering of militant Black nationalist organizations testified to his impact on the ghettos, concludes the editor.

134. Foner, Philip S., Editor. The Voice of Black America: Major Speeches by Negroes in the United States, 1797-1973. NY: Capricorn Books, 1973. Vol. 2. Malcolm X, pp. 343, 369-385, 387, 397-399, 418, 500.

Malcolm X's "The Ballot or the Bullet," Ossie Davis' "Malcolm Was Our Manhood, Our Living Black Manhood." It was also stated that Malcolm X's voice was the voice of pride for the Black poor.

135. Ford, Nick Aaron. Black Studies: Threat-Or-Challenger. Port Washington, NY: Kennikat Press, 1973. Malcolm X, pp. 14, 21, 207. It was stated that Malcolm X publicly repudiated the Black Muslims doctrine of Black racism when he returned from Mecca in 1964.

136. Franklin, John Hope, Editor. Color and Race. Boston, MA: Houghton Mifflin Co., 1968, Malcolm X, pp. 337-338.

In David Lowenthal's article, "Race and Color in the West Indies," he argues that a surprising number of Malcolm X's ideologicaly successors, advocates of "Black Power," "Black Nationalism," or, more fundamentally, Black self-esteem, are West Indian-born.

137. ______________. From Slavery to Freedom: A History of Negro America. NY: Alfred A. Knopf, 1980. Malcolm X, pp. 413, 484, 487.

Professor Franklin asserts that Malcolm X was the ablest and most eloquent spokesman for the Black Muslims.

138. ______________ and Isidore Starr. The Negro in Twentieth Century America: A Reader on the Struggle for Civil Rights. NY: Vintage Books, 1967. Malcolm X, pp. 15-16.

Malcolm X's "As Seen By a Bright Schoolboy" is discussed.

139. Franklin, Raymond S. and Solomon Resnik. The Political Economy of Racism. NY: Holt, Rinehart and Winston, 1973. Malcolm X, pp. 112, 127, 178-181, 183.

The writers surmise that Malcolm X came to the same realization that the Marxists before him had come to: that there is a causal link between capitalism and racism.

140. Freed, Donald. Agony in New Haven: The Trial of Bobby Seale, Ericka Huggins, and The Black Panther Party. NY: Simon & Schuster, 1973. Malcolm X, pp. 18-20, 22, 38-40, 54, 103, 112-115, 191-221, 238, 309.

The writer suggests that the life and death of Malcolm X was a personification of the struggle between the past and the future, the religious and the material, the national and the international. He also discusses Bobby Seale's opinion of Malcolm X.

141. Fulk, Bryan. Black Struggle: A History of the Negro in America. NY: Delacorte Press, 1969. Malcolm X, pp. 315, 316, 317, 318, 319, 320.

The writer states that Malcolm X and Martin Luther King, Jr. had used markedly different approaches toward the same ultimate goal -- the achievement by the Black people of a life of human dignity.

142. Gardner, Carl. Andrew Young: A Biography. NY: Drake Publishers, Inc., 1978. Malcolm X, pp. 89-90.

The author declares that Malcolm X, at SNCC's invitation, came to Selma, Alabama and this prestaged an escalation which made Andrew Young feel uneasy. Young could not be certain of what would happen with the volatile Malcolm in Selma.

143. Garraty, John A., Editor. Encyclopedia of American Biography. NY: Harper & Row, 1974. Malcolm X, pp. 723-724.

This short biographical sketch of Malcolm X was written by his biographer, Peter Goldman.

144. Garvey, Amy Jacques. Black Power in America: Marcus Garvey's Impact on Jamaica and Africa. Kingston, Jamaica: The Author, 1968.

Marcus Garvey's widow declares that there is a connection between her husband's teaching and the philosophy of Elijah Muhammad and Malcolm X.

145. Gayle, Addison, Jr. The Black Situation. NY: Dell Publishing Co., 1970. Malcolm X, pp. 23, 44-45, 91, 135, 156, 183.

The author suggests that an examination of the rhetoric of such leaders during the Malcolm X years will convince even the most disinterested observer that Negro leaders, reflecting white concern, had nominated Malcolm X public enemy number one.

146. Gilliam, Reginald Earl, Jr. Black Political Development: An Advocacy Analysis. NY: Dunellen Publishing Co., 1975. Malcolm X, pp. 12, 183, 184, 186-187, 276.

Author suggests that Malcolm X's thesis, that aiding the Democrats in being a majority party, Blacks were supporting the same elements that oppressed them.

147. Graham, Hugh David, et. al., Editors. Violence: The Crisis of American Confidence. Baltimore, MD: John Hopkins Press, 1971. Malcolm X, pp. 110, 117-118.

There is one article in this collection by Leon Higginbotham, Jr., entitled, "The Black Prisoner: America's Caged Canary." He discusses Malcolm X and how he became a Black Muslim while he was in prison.

148. Grant, Joanne. Black Protest: History, Documents, and Analyses 1619 to the Present. NY: St. Martin's Press, 1968. Malcolm X, pp. 374, 426, 448-452, 457-459.

"Malcolm X at the Audubon," and "Malcolm was a Man" by Ossie Davis are included in this collection.

149. Gregory, Dick, with James R. McGraw. Up From Nigger. NY: Stein and Day, 1976. Malcolm X, pp. 27-29, 84-87, 153, 186.

The writer discusses his friendship with Malcolm X.

150. Grier, William H. and Price M. Cobbs. Black Rage. NY: Basic Books, 1968. Malcolm X, pp. 168, 200-202.

The writers conclude: "Malcolm's meaning for us lies in his fearless demand for truth and his evolution from a petty criminal to an international statesman - accomplished by a Black man against odds of terrible magnitude-in America. His message was his life, not his words, and Malcolm knew it."

151. Grove Press. A Discussion Guide for the Autobiography of Malcolm X. NY: Grove Press, 1965. 12 pp.

This guide is offered as an aid to a meaningful exploration of the reality of life in America. The study of Malcolm X throws strong light on the central problem of our time.

152. Hale, Frank W. Jr., Compiler. The Cry for Freedom: An Anthology of the Best That Has Been Said and Written on Civil Rights Since 1954. NY: A.S. Barnes and Co., 1969. Malcolm X, pp. 377-391.

Malcolm X's speech, "The Black Revolution," is included in this collection.

153. Hall, Raymond L., Editor. Black Separatism and Social Reality: Rhetoric and Reason. NY: Pergamon Press, Inc., 1977. Malcolm X, pp. xiv, 7, 30, 31, 32, 35, 36, 42, 48, 63, 65, 69, 77, 78, 95, 101, 102, 115, 131, 144, 146, 147, 150, 161, 166, 183, 192, 194, 195, 199, 202, 215, 218.

Malcolm X is discussed as a separatist and as a Pan-Africanist.

154. ________________________. Black Separatism in the United States. Hanover, NH: University Press of New England, 1978. Malcolm X, (El Hajj Malik El Shabazz, Malcolm Little): Black middle class, 108; Black Panther Party, 193-194; Black Power, 9, 116; Core, 181; death, 108, 132; early background, 90-91; economic program, 117; Elijah Muhammad, 105, 107; federal government, 169; integration, 178; internal colonialism, 148, 149; James Farmer, 180; nation of Islam, 104, 107, 177, 179, 184, 193, 217, 219; organization of Afro-American Unity, 189; ouster from Muslims, 107, 184, 192; Pan-Africanism 204; philosophy, 105-108, 122, 123; RNA, 191; separate state, 132; rise to prominence, 4, 94, 104; SNCC, 184, 185; separatism, 97, 193; white racism, 218.

Malcolm X is discussed throughout this book.

155. Hamilton, Charles V. The Black Preacher in America. NY: William Morrow & Co., 1972. Malcolm X, pp. 17, 81, 83, 84, 85, 86, 87, 133, 134, 135, 171, 176-177, 193.

The author states that Malcolm X's entire life was one of constant transition. He concludes that in many ways this is the story of Black people, and it is appropriate that the story should be reflected in the life of one of their most dynamic preachers in modern times.

156. ___________________. The Black Experience in American Politics. NY: G. P. Putnam's Sons, 1973. Malcolm X, pp. 165-170.

"God's Judgment of White America." Speech delivered December, 1963, New York City.

157. Harding, Vincent. There Is a River: The Black Struggle for Freedom in America. NY: Harcourt Brace Jovanovich, 1981. Malcolm X, pp. xiv-xv, xxi, 189.

The writer describes Malcolm X by declaring: "The love he bore to his people, the overwhelming power of his black consciousness, and the force and integrity of his spirit offered a powerful testimony to the possibilities of human transformation."

158. Haskins, James. Profiles in Black Power. Garden City, NY: Doubleday & Co., 1972. Malcolm X, pp. 103-122.

The writer concludes: "Although (Malcolm X) he did not live long enough to develop an over-all philosophy for the liberation of Black people in America, his ideas and influence have provided a firm basis for a new Black consciousness in America and for new Black leaders to carry on what he began."

159. Heath, G. Louis. Off The Pigs!: The History and Literature of the Black Panther Party. Metuchen, NJ: Scarecrow Press, Inc., 1976. Malcolm X, pp. 25, 26, 27, 28, 37, 41, 42, 149.

The author surmises that the patron saint of the Black Panther groups which sprang up in the urban ghettos of the North was the late Malcolm X. Huey Newton described the members of the Black Panther Party as "heirs of Malcolm X."

160. Hedgeman, Anna Arnold. The Gift of Chaos: Decades of American Discontent. NY: Oxford University Press, 1977. Malcolm X, pp. 72-74, 91, 177, 191, 229.

Various references are made to Malcolm X throughout this book. The author recalls that she heard Malcolm X on a street corner in Harlem protesting Martin Luther King, Jr.'s nonviolent stance with the words, "Defend yourself when attacked - that's the American way!"

161. Helmreich, William B. The Black Crusaders: A Case Study of Black Militant Organization. NY: Harper & Row, Publishers, 1973. Malcoom X, pp. 7, 14, 16, 24, 30.

The writer points out that by 1964 one of the most popular Black leaders in the Black Movement was Malcolm X. He concludes: "The emergence of Malcolm X as a national leader in the 1960's was indicative of the widening influence of black militancy, which, in its many forms, soon became an integral part of the modern Black Movement."

162. Hendin, Herbert. Black Suicide. NY: Basic Books, 1969. Malcolm X, pp. 125, 142.

The author declares that the ease with which ghetto life encourages moving in antisocial directions has been graphically described by Malcolm X and others.

163. Herbers, John. The Lost Priority: What Happened to the Civil Rights Movement in America? NY: Funk & Wagnalls, 1970. Malcolm X, pp. xvii, 66, 67, 68, 198, 204, 216, 218 - 219.

Malcolm X's role in the Civil Rights Movement is discussed.

164. ____________. The Black Dilemma. NY: John Day Co., 1973. Malcolm X, pp. 36, 46, 49, 52-54.

The writer concludes that Malcolm X and others all wanted to provide national leadership and a viable program for the lower-class Blacks in the cities who would never follow nonviolence, but none of their movements could be sustained.

165. Hercules, Frank. American Society and Black Revolution. NY: Harcourt Brace Jovanovich, Inc., 1972. Malcolm X, pp. 7, 9, 10, 44, 199, 288, 289, 290, 291, 292, 293, 294, 295, 296, 297, 298, 299, 303, 341, 342, 343, 344, 345, 350-354, 378.

Author asserts that it is safe to say that Malcolm X intended nothing so visionary, so impracticable, as a Black state within the comity of the United States. Malcolm X is also compared to Adam Clayton Powell, Jr., Marcus Garvey, and Martin Luther King, Jr.

166. Hernton, Calvin C. White Paper for White Americans. Garden City, NY: Doubleday & Co., 1966. Section two of chapter 3 is entitled "Another Man Done Gone: The Death of Malcolm X," pp. 97-104.

The writer concludes: "He was the rare kind of personage of the masses which societies produce once every fifty to a hundred years....All that is left to us now is to bury him, and perhaps utter...ANOTHER MAN DONE GONE."

167. Hickey, Neil and Ed Edwin. Adam Clayton Powell and the Politics of Race. NY: Fleet Publishing Corp., 1965. Malcolm X, pp. 6, 8, 9, 11, 116, 155, 162, 163, 164, 165, 166, 170, 236, 251, 262, 270, 271, 275, 278, 289, 297.

The writers state that a peculiar pattern of self-destructiveness came into focus with Adam Clayton Powell's embracing of Malcolm X and the concomitant espousal of the cause of separatism over the black-white cooperation.

168. Hill, Roy L. Rhetoric of Racial Revolt. Denver, CO: Golden Bell Press, 1964. Malcolm X, pp. 304-317.

"Malcolm X Proclaims Muhammad As Man of the Hour." Speech delivered at Yale University, New Haven, Conn., October, 1960.

169. Holden, Matthew, Jr. The Politics of the Black "Nation." NY: Chandler Publishing Co., 1973. Malcolm X, pp. 102, 103, 116, 117, 122.

Writer discusses Malcolm X Society, Malcolm X Community College and Malcolm X University.

170. Hughes, Langston, Milton Meltzer, and C. Eric Lincoln. A Pictoral History of Black Americans. NY: Crown Publishers, Inc., 1956. Malcolm X, pp. 5, 340.

He is reported to have stated: "We are all black, different shades of black," state the writers.

171. ________________ and Milton Meltzer. A Pictoral History of the Negro in America. NY: Crown Publishers, Inc., 1968. Malcolm X, pp. 330, 331, 368.

Malcolm X was instrumental in setting up Black Muslims Mosques all across the country in the late 1950's and early 1960's, state the authors.

172. Imair, Brother. War in America. Detroit, MI: Malcolm X Society, 1968.

This society named after its founder, Malcolm X, states that it wanted the American government to support and recognize a new Black nation-state.

173. Institute of the Black World. Black Analysis for the Seventies. Atlanta, GA: Institute of the Black World, 1973. Malcolm X, pp. 1-5.

There is an article entitled, "The Meaning of Malcolm X for the 70's," in this work.

174. Jackson, Florence. Blacks in America: 1954-1979. NY: Franklin Watts, 1980. Malcolm X, pp. 30-32.

It was stated that Malcolm X was one of the most influential men in the Black Muslim sect. He became a major influence to many groups within the Black community as he preached unity in order to achieve the liberation of Black people.

175. Johnson, Harry A., Editor. Negotiating the Mainstream: A Survey of the Afro-American Experience. Chicago, IL: American Library Association, 1978. Malcolm X, pp. 37, 59, 188, 189, 197, 205, 214.

The author states that largely because of Malcolm's analysis and his consummate skill in articulating it, the Nation of Islam, during the early 1960's, was considered by the United States Government to be a dangerous or subversive organization.

176. Jones, Leroi, Editor. Black Fire. NY: William Morrow & Co., 1968. Malcolm X, pp. 32-38.

There is one article by Leslie Alexander Lacy entitled, "African Responses to Malcolm X."

177. ________________. Home: Social Essays. NY: William Morrow & Co., 1966. Malcolm X, pp. 238-250.

"The Legacy of Malcolm X and The Coming of the Black Nation" is included in this work.

178. Jordan, June. Civil Wars. Boston, MA: Beacon Press, 1981. Malcolm X, pp, xviii, 15, 19, 42, 85-86.

Miss Jordan concludes: "...it is tragic and ridiculous to choose between Malcolm X and Dr. (Martin Luther) King: each of them hurled himself against a quite different aspect of our predicament, and both of them, literally, gave their lives to our ongoing struggle."

179. Justice, Blair. Violence in the City. Fort Worth, TX: Texas Christian University Press, 1969. Malcolm X, pp. 114, 123, 126 - 127.

The writer gives the profile of one Black Muslim who felt closer to Malcolm X than to Elijah Muhammad.

180. Katz, William Loren. Eyewitness: The Negro in American History. NY: Pitman Publishing Corp., 1967. Malcolm X, pp. 489, 507 - 508.

"Malcolm X Explains Black Nationalism." This was a statement delivered by Malcolm X to a New York Press Conference, March 12, 1964.

181. ____________________. Teachers' Guide to American Negro History. Chicago, IL: Quadrangle Books, 1968. Malcolm X, pp. 162, 164 - 165.

Writer states Malcolm X was a spokesman for the Black Muslims and became the symbol of Black Nationalism.

182. Keil, Charles. Urban Blues. Chicago, IL: University of Chicago Press, 1966. Malcolm X, pp. 20, 42, 183, 193.

The writer points out: "As Malcolm X saw so very clearly integration' is neither the issue nor the answer. Freedom is the issue. Freedom is never given or granted - it is won."

183. Killian, Lewis M. The Impossible Revolution?: Black Power and the American Dream. NY: Random House, 1968. Malcolm X, pp. xi, xii, 94, 98, 155, 156, 167, 183n.

The author surmises that had Malcolm X lived, he might have been the type of leader who, with his lieutenants, would have the nucleus for the building of a revolutionary army.

184. ________________. The Impossible Revolution, Phase II: Black Power and the American Dream. NY: Random House, 1975. Malcolm X, pp. 83, 86, 135, 164-165.

The writer surmises that the Black Muslims and the defectors who had followed Malcolm X out of the sect were the best-known proponents of Black Nationalism, and retaliatory violence. He also discusses Malcolm's influence on the Black Power Movement.

185. Kluger, Richard. Simple Justice: The History of Brown v. Board of Education and Black America's Struggle for Equality. NY: Vintage Books, 1975. Malcolm X, pp. 758, 759, 763.

The author states: "During Lyndon Johnson's first months in the White House, Malcolm X demeaned him as 'a Southern cracker - that's all he is'."

186. Kofsky, Frank. Black Nationalism and the Revolution in Music. NY: Pathfinder Press, 1970. Chapter 13 is entitled "Black Revolution and Black Music: The Career of Malcolm X," pp. 249-262.

The writer concludes: "Though his death cannot be too much mourned, it is still no meager comfort to know that where the vanguard leads, there too shall the remainder of the columns march."

187. Kovel, Joel. White Racism: A Psycho-History. NY: Pantheon Books, 1970. Malcolm X, pp. 13, 242.

Author called Malcolm X "A contemporary creative spirit."

188. Lecky, Robert S. and H. Elliott Wright. Black Manifesto: Religion, Racism and Reparations. NY: Sheed and Ward, 1969. Malcolm X, p. 80.

The writers state that when Malcolm X journeyed to Mecca, he saw human "solidarity and kinship."

189. Lester, Julius. Key List Mailing: Selected Documents of Current and Interest in the Civil Rights Movement. San Francisco, CA: Office of Student Non-Violent Coordinating Committee, December 11, 1966.

One document includes "The Angry Children of Malcolm X," the essence of which is that Malcolm X served as a source of both inspiration and ideology to many young Black nationalists.

190. Levine, Lawrence W. Black Culture and Black Consciousness: Afro-American Folk Thought from Slavery to Freedom. NY: Oxford University Press, 1977. Malcolm X, pp. 291-292, 435, 438.

The author points out that when Malcolm X was a young man in New York he followed the practice of many lower-class Blacks and Black entertainers and "conked" or straightened his hair through the painful process of applying lye.

191. Levy, Felice. Obituaries on File. Vol. 1. NY: Facts on File, 1979. Malcolm X, p. 374.

Compiler gives a short obituary on Malcolm X. She called him founder and leader of an extremist Black Nationalist movement.

192. Lewis, Anthony. Portrait of a Decade. NY: Random House, 1953. Malcolm X, p. 187.

Malcolm X denounced Martin Luther King, Jr. and his strategy of non-violent demonstrations in this work.

193. Lincoln, C. Eric. The Black Muslims in America. Boston, MA: Beacon Press, 1961. Malcolm X, pp. 4, 7, 18, 19, 31, 67, 68, 69, 71, 82, 87, 95, 96, 97, 110, 112, 113, 115, 116, 130, 132, 134, 137, 138, 139, 141, 148, 150, 151, 154, 157, 166, 169, 172, 173, 175, 178, 183, 189, 190, 190, 191, 192, 193, 195, 196, 197, 198, 204, 205, 207, 208, 222-225.

The writer discusses the role of Malcolm X in the Nation of Islam. The author also lists the several interviews that he had with Malcolm X.

194. ________________. My Face Is Black. Boston, MA: Beacon Press, 1964. Chapter 4 is entitled "Mood Ebony: The Meaning of Malcolm X," pp. 91-117, 121, 127, 128, 132 - 133.

He concludes: "If Malcolm X means anything, it is that America has but a little time to learn that meaning of color, which is, that it has no meaning."

195. ________________. Sounds of the Struggle: Persons and Perspectives in Civil Rights. NY: William Morrow & Co., 1967. Malcolm X, pp. 36, 47, 62-63, 66-67, 85, 114, 146-152.

Chapter 11 is entitled "The Meaning of Malcolm X." Dr. Lincoln concludes: "Malcolm X must be taken for what he was. He was a remarkably gifted and charismatic leader whose hatreds and resentments symbolized the dreadful stamp of the black ghetto, but a man whose philosophies of racial determination and whose commitments to violence made him unacceptable as a serious participant in peaceful change...."

196. ________________. The Negro Pilgrimage in America: The Coming of Age of the Black-Americans. NY: Frederick A. Praeger, 1969. Malcolm X, pp. 145, 150, 151, 190, 193.

States that perhaps the most striking and interesting figure to emerge from the Black Muslim Movement was Malcolm X. He concludes: "Malcolm X is a symbol of the two alternatives Americans face today: A peaceful solution to the racial problem, with Negroes and whites working earnestly together; or hatred, violence, and open warfare."

197. Lomax, Louis E. When the Word is Given: A Report on Elijah Muhammad, Malcolm X and the Black Muslim World. Cleveland, IL: World Publishing Co., 1963. 223 pp.

Five speeches by Malcolm X are included.

198. ________________. To Kill a Black Man. Los Angeles, CA: Holloway House Publishing Co., 1968.

Part of this book discusses the life and times of Malcolm X and part of it discusses Martin Luther King,Jr.

199. Low, W. Augustus and Virgil A. Clift, Editors. Encyclopedia of Black America. NY: McGraw-Hill Book Co., 1981. Malcolm X, pp. 182, 270, 345, 418. 529, 544, 545, 610, 700.

Many references are made to Malcolm X throughout this work.

200. Loye, David. The Healing of a Nation. NY: W. W. Norton & Co., 1971. Malcolm X, pp. 91, 125, 207, 253, 259, 264, 265, 266, 274.

The author suggests that Malcolm X was a forerunner of Black Power. He also surmises that though his efforts were laughed at, Malcolm X is credited with being militancy's chief ideologue.

201. Loyer, Yves. Black Power (Etude et Documents). Paris: Etudes et Documentation Internationales, 1968. Malcolm X, pp. 10, 26, 65, 75, 128, 158, 206, 222.

Writer discusses Malcolm X and Separatism. Also the SNCC and Malcolm X.

202. McKissick, Floyd. Three-Fifths of a Man. NY: Macmillan Co., 1969. Malcolm X, pp. 128, 132, Contribution to Black America, pp. 128-131, death of, 130.

The author states that the cause of the Muslims has been advanced by two of the most prominent and admired Black men of the twentieth century - Malcolm X and Muhammad Ali. It was also surmised that although Malcolm left the Muslims before his death, while a minister in that faith he brought their cause to the attention of America.

203. Major, Reginald. A Panther is a Black Cat: A Study in Depth of the Black Panther Party - Its Origins, Its Goals, and Its Struggle for Survival. NY: William Morrow & Co., 1971. Malcolm X, pp. 65, 66, 67, 142, 160.

Author states that the Black Panthers and every revolutionary Black orientation in America readily acknowledges Malcolm X as the most important influence on their thinking and activities.

204. Marable, Manning. From the Grassroots: Essays Toward Afro-American Liberation. Boston, MA: South End Press, 1980. Malcolm X, pp. 1, 82, 83, 101, 112, 117, 148, 149, 181, 211, 242.

The author concludes that "drawing inspiration from Malcolm X's critical search for a grassroots agenda for Black people in 1964 and early 1965, these essays attempt to embrace the totality of the black experience of the nineteen seventies and examine many aspects of white American culture and political society."

205. Masotte, Louis Hetal. A time To Burn?: An Evaluation of the Present Crisis in Race Relations. Chicago, IL: Rand McNally & Company, 1969. Malcolm X, pp. 9-10, 39, 40, 41, 50, 51, 60.

The author declared that Malcolm X's language had been sophisticated in its analysis of corruption in politics.

206. Meier, August and Elliott Rudwick, Editors. Black Protest in the Sixties. Chicago, IL: Quadrangle Books, 1970. Malcolm X, pp. 14, 15, 39, 40, 69, 136, 143, 144, 145, 146, 152, 167, 233-239, 248.

Various references are made to Malcolm X and his role in the Nation of Islam.

207. ______________ et al Editors. Black Protest Thought in the Twentieth Century. Indianapolis, IN: Bobbs-Merrill Co., 1971. Second Edition. Malcolm X (Malcolm Little) pp. xlv, xlviii, 355, 387-396, 404-409, 412, 413, 452, 469-474, 479, 486, 497, 500, 503, 526, 565, 567, 577, 580.

Various references are made to Malcolm X throughout this work.

208. ______________________________. CORE: A Study in the Civil Rights Movement: 1942-1968. Urbana, IL: University of Illinois Press, 1075. Malcolm X: influence on CORE members, pp. 202, 204, 206, 303, 331, 332, 374, 429; debates Bayard Rustin, pp. 206, 207; debates Floyd McKissick, p. 207; forms Organization of Afro-American Unity, p. 297; address Cleveland CORE meeting on "The Ballot or the Bullet,", p. 300; mentioned on pp. 254, 318.

Various references are made to Malcolm X throughout this work.

209. Metcalf, George R. Black Profiles. NY: McGraw-Hill Book Co., 1970. Expanded Edition. Malcolm X, pp. 335-368.

The writer concludes that the supreme tragedy of Malcolm X's death was that he was so misrepresented and misunderstood during his life.

210. Mezu, S. Okechukwu. Black Leaders of the Centuries. Buffalo, NY: Black Academy Press, 1970. Malcolm X, pp. 281-291.

The writer gives a short overview of Malcolm X's life and calls him one of the greatest Black leaders of the centuries.

211. Mitchell, Loften. Black Drama. NY: Hawthorn Books, 1967. Malcolm X, pp. 36, 54, 178, 184.

The author suggests that northern leadership scream, shudder and denounced Malcolm X when he drew a large personal following from Harlem.

212. Moquin, Wayne, Editor. Makers of America-Emergent Minorities 1955-1970. Chicago, IL: Encyclopaedia Britannica Educational Corp., 1971. Malcolm X, pp. 43-46, 185.

Editor included Malcolm X's "Advice to the Youth of Mississippi." It was reprinted from Malcolm X Speaks, edited by George Breitman.

213. Morsbach, Mabel. The Negro in American Life. NY: Harcourt Brace & World, Inc., 1966. Malcolm X, p. 217.

The writer states that with the aid of his sons and a young follower, Malcolm X, Elijah Muhammad transformed the Black Muslims from a small cult in the slums of Detroit to an elaborate national organization.

214. Moses, Wilson J. Blacks, Messiahs, and Uncle Toms: Social and Literary Manipulations of Religious Myth. University Park, PA: Pennsylvania State University Press, 1982.

Various references are made to Malcolm X throughout this book. The writer also compared Malcolm X's leadership role in the Civil Rights Movement with that of Martin Luther King, Jr.

215. Muhammad, Elijah. Message to the Blackman in America. Chicago, IL: Muhammad Mosque of Islam No. 2, 1965.

Various references are made to Malcolm X throughout this work.

216. ________________. The Fall of America. Chicago, IL: Muhammad's Temple of Islam No. 2, 1973. Malcolm X, pp. 94, 95, 96, 206 - 207.

The author states that Malcolm was a doublecrosser and was used by the white man against him.

217. Mullen, Robert W. Rhetorical Strategies of Black Americans. Washington, DC: University Press of America, 1980. Malcolm X, pp. 30-35.

The author concludes that for Malcolm, the goals of freedom, justice, and the "good life," were the same as the assimilationist goals, but he could not believe integration was the best route to those goals.

218. Muse, Benjamin. The American Negro Revolution: From Nonviolence to Black Power, 1963-1967. Bloomington,IN: Indiana University Press, 1968. Malcolm X, pp. 13, 25, 115, 160-161, 235.

The writer states that Malcolm X was a man of considerable ability and magnetism.

219. Nazel, Joseph. Paul Robeson: Biography of a Proud Man. Los Angeles, CA: Holloway House Publishing Co., 1980. Malcolm X, pp. 176 - 177.

Malcolm comments on Africa as the motherland for Black people.

220. Newton, Huey P. To Die for the People: The Writings of Huey P. Newton. NY: Random House, 1972. Malcolm X, pp. 90, 91, 93 - 94.

The writer states that the choice offered by the heirs of Malcolm X to the endorsed spokesmen is to repudiate the oppressor and to crawl back to their own people and earn a speedy reprieve or face a merciless, speedy and most timely execution for treason and being "too wrong for too long."

221. Osofsky, Gilbert. The Burden of Race: A Documentary History of Negro-White Relations in America. NY: Harper & Row, Publishers, 1967. Malcolm X, pp. 427, 594; on Black Nationalism, 595-608; on Politics, 598-608.

Various references to Malcolm X are made throughout this book.

222. Paris, Peter J. Black Leaders in Conflict: Joseph H. Jackson, Martin Luther King, Jr., Malcolm X, and Adam Clayton Powell, Jr. NY: Pilgrim Press, 1978. 254 pp. Malcolm X, pp. 140-174, 187-189, 191-192, 195-196, 202-220.

It was stated that Malcolm X's basic principle governing his understanding of social change was racial self-determination. In his thought, racial self-determination is the first principle of any nationalism, and since it is sought by Blacks, it must entail radical change in the American societal system.

223. Parks, Gordon. Born Black. Philadelphia, PA: J. B. Lippincott Co., 1971. Malcolm X, pp. 51-62. Chapter 3 is entitled "The Death of Malcolm X," pp. 25-50, concerning the Black Muslims and Malcolm X.

224. Parris, Guichard and Lester Brooks. Blacks in the City: A History of the National Urban League. Boston, MA: Little, Brown and Co., 1971. Malcolm X, pp. 384, 415, 425, 449, 462.

Various references to Malcolm X and the National Urban League's view of him. Authors state that Rap Brown and Stokely were the offspring of Malcolm X's most fevered exhortations to reject and suspect everything white.

225. Parsons, Talcott and Kenneth B. Clark, Editors. The Negro American. Boston, MA: Houghton Mifflin Company, 1965. Malcolm X, pp. 35, 46, 245, 246, 640; murder of, 655.

Article in this work stated that the newspaper, The Spark, accused the American ruling class of assassinating Malcolm X because nine African states, influenced by him, are to raise the question of American race discrimination in the United Nations.

226. Peeks, Edward. The Long Struggle for Black Power. NY: Charles Scribner's Sons, 1971. Malcolm X, (Shabazz; Malcolm Little), pp. 21, 263-266.

Author surmises that Malcolm X was credited with bringing Muhammad Ali into the Nation of Islam.

227. Pinkney, Alphonso. Black Americans. Second Edition. Englewood Cliffs, NJ: Prentice-Hall, 1975. Malcolm X, pp. 188n. 18, 189, 202n. 45, 207, 212n. 5, 213, 224, 225; ideas of, 188, 189; role of in Black nationalism, 212, 213, and Third World Movement.

Various references are made to Malcolm X throughout this work.

228. ________________. Red, Black, and Green: Black Nationalism in the United States. Cambridge, MA: Cambridge University Press, 1976. Malcolm X, pp. 5, 64-75, 98, 190-195.

Chapter 4 is entitled "Malcolm X and the Rise of Contemporary Nationalism." The writer called Malcolm X one of the most influential thinkers of the twentieth century. He also declares that Malcolm X was totally dedicated to the liberation of Afro-Americans.

229. ________________. The Committed: White Activists in the Civil Rights Movement. New Haven, CT: College & University Press Publishers, 1968. Malcolm X, pp. 135, 230; as civil rights leader, 139; attitudes of white activists towards, 143-145.

Author states that what Malcolm X advocated was not the initiation of violence on the part of Negroes, but rather, armed self-defense in an effort to protect oneself from violent attacks by racists. Mr. Pinkney declares that this fact is little understood by Americans, although he was always clear on the point.

230. Ploski, Harry A., et. al., Editors. Reference Library of Black America. Vol. 1. NY: Bellwether Publishing Co., 1971. Malcolm X, pp. 48, 105, 109.

Editors discuss Malcolm X's assassination. They also called him a charismatic Black leader.

231. ______________ and Ernest Kaiser, Editors. AFRO USA: A Reference Work on the Black Experience. NY: Bellwether Publishing Co., 1971. Malcolm X, pp. 39, 232, 237, 372, 394; assassination of, p. 38; struggle for freedom, p. 543.

Various references are made to Malcolm X throughout this work.

232. Powell, Adam Clayton, Jr. Adam By Adam: The Autobiography of Adam Clayton Powell, Jr. NY: Dial Press, 1971. Malcolm X, pp. 243-244.

The writer points out Malcolm X, one of the great minds we Black people lost, was a dear friend of his. He states that he was able to give him a better understanding of his religion and he urged Malcolm X to go to the Arab countries and if possible to Mecca to find out what Islam really was.

233. Rein, Irving J., Editor. The Relevant Rhetoric: Principles of Public Speaking Through Case Studies. NY: Free Press, 1969.

Malcolm X's "The Ballot or the Bullet" speech is included in this collection.

234. Revolutionary Action Movement (RAM). Why Malcolm X Died: An Analysis. NY: The Liberator, April, 1965. Malcolm X, pp. 9-11.

The writers argue that Malcolm X became a threat to "Charlie" when he broke from the Nation of Islam because of his statements which expressed the sentiment of Black America and his attempt to organize a Black national movement. He immediately put himself in danger by attempting to organize the Black community for self-defense..., declare the authors.

235. Rich, Andrea L. and Arthur L. Smith. Rhetoric of Revolution: Samuel Adams, Emma Goldman, Malcolm X. Durham, NC: Moore Publishing Co., 1971. Malcolm X, pp. 143-213, 260-293.

The section on Malcolm X is entitled, "Architect of Black Revolution." Two of Malcolm X's speeches, "On Unity" and "The Ballot or the Bullet," are also included.

236. Richardson, Ben and William A. Fahey. Great Black Americans. NY: Thomas Y. Crowell Co., 1976. Malcolm X, pp. 173, 218-229, 239.

The writers state that Malcolm X had experienced a spiritual rebirth in the Holy Land. And on the way back to America, travelling through Ghana and Nigeria, he experienced another kind of renewal, a discovery of his cultural roots, suggest the authors.

237. Romero, Patricia W., Editor. In Black America: 1968, The Year of Awakening. Washington, DC: United Publishing Corp., 1969. Malcolm X, pp. 45-46, 62, 92, 105, 312, 323.

The editor points out that young militants had been developing an ideological stance since 1964 that incorporated more of the philosophy of Malcolm X than of Martin Luther King, Jr.

238. Ross, James Robert, Editor. The War Within: Violence or Nonviolence in the Black Revolution. NY: Sheed and Ward, 1971. Malcolm X, pp. 37-58.

"The Lex Talionis" by Malcolm X. The editor surmises that Malcolm's justification for violence is the ancient lex talionis, the law of an eye for an eye and a tooth for a tooth.

239. Rush, Theressa G., et. al. Black American Writers Past and Present: A Biographical and Bibliographical Dictionary. Metuchen, NJ: Scarecrow Press, 1975. Vol. 2. Malcolm X, pp. 524-526.

Three page bio-bibliography of works by and about Malcolm X is included in this collection.

240. Rustin, Bayard. Down the Line: The Collected Writings of Bayard Rustin. Chicago, IL: Quadrangle Books, 1971. Malcolm X, pp. 117, 132-139, 157.

The writer includes his review of The Autobiography of Malcolm X that appeared in the November 14, 1965 issue of the Sunday Herald Tribune. He declares that "there is much that we can learn about the sickness and the cure from Malcolm X."

241. Santa Barbara County Board of Education. The Emerging Minorities in America: A Resource Guide for Teachers. Santa Barbara, CA: American Bibliographical Center-CLIO Press, 1972. Malcolm X, pp. 81 - 82.

The authors state that Malcolm X was a prime leader of the modern Black nationalist movement in the United States.

242. Scheer, Robert, Editor. Eldridge Cleaver: Post-Prison Writings and Speeches. NY: Ramparts Books, 1969. Malcolm X, pp. ix, xi, 15, 17, 23, 24, 27, 28, 32, 37, 38, 52, 62, 66, 67, 69, 71, 73, 78, 178.

Malcolm X is mentioned in several of Eldridge Cleaver's post-prison writings and speeches. In one speech, "The Decline of the Black Muslims," he stated one of the major reasons for the decline of the Muslims in prisons was the split in the Nation of Islam that developed over the callous ouster and subsequent murder of Malcolm X, who was the universal hero of Black prisoners.

243. Schlesinger, Arthur M. Jr. *A Thousand Days: John F. Kennedy in the White House*. NY: Houghton Mifflin Co., 1965. Malcolm X, pp. 958, 961.

James Baldwin describes meeting with Malcolm X and Elijah Muhammad; while rejecting their racism, he unwillingly acknowledged their appeal.

244. Schuchter, Arnold. *Reparations: The Black Manifesto and its Challenge to White America*. Philadelphia, PA: J. B. Lippincott Co., 1970. Malcolm X, pp. 80, 90.

States that Malcolm X's affirmation of Black identity and his demand for either an African homeland or a "separate territory here in the Western hemisphere" is a variation on the theme of Black liberation from white oppression.

245. ________________. *White Power/Black Freedom Planning the Future of Urban America*. Boston, MA: Beacon Press, 1968. Malcolm X, pp. 2, 8, 96. His view compared to Martin Luther King, Jr., pp. 569, 573.

Various references are made to Malcolm X throughout this work.

246. Scott, Benjamin. *The Coming of the Black Man*. Boston, MA: Beacon Press, 1969.

This work was dedicated "To the memory of Martin Luther King, Jr. and Malcolm X."

247. Scott, Robert L. and Wayne Brockriede, Editors. *The Rhetoric of Black Power*. NY: Harper and Row, 1969. Malcolm X, pp. 3, 132, 133, 137, 138, 142, 144, 192.

Malcolm X is mentioned throughout this collection of speeches and articles. It was pointed out: "Malcolm X is dead, but his words echo in the speeches of Stokely Carmichael, H. Rap Brown, John Hulett, Harry Edwards, Herman B. Ferguson, Fred Brooks, and others,"

248. Sherwin, Mark. *The Extremists*. NY: St. Martin's Press, 1963. Malcolm X, pp. 190-192, 210-212.

The writer discusses Malcolm's role in the Black Muslims. He also points out "It is (in 1962) already accepted in New York's Harlem that Malcolm X is in a position to decide who will succeed Representative Adam Clayton Powell when he retires. Many political leaders of both colors have shown renewed interest and respect for the actions and pronouncements of Malcolm X."

249. Sidran, Ben. *Black Talk*. NY: Holt, Rinehart and Winston, 1971. Malcolm X, pp. xv, 133, 140, 146, 148, 155, 185.

Various references are made between Malcolm X and John Coltrane. Both were radicals, but in different ways. Malcolm was a radical leader and Coltrane was radical in his music.

250. Silberman, Charles E. Crisis in Black and White. NY: Random House, 1964. Malcolm X, pp. 55, 56, 57, 68, 111, 150, 152, 153, 154, 155, 156, 157, 158, 159, 161, 162.

States that psychiatric social workers in Harlem Hospital in New York, amazed by the Muslims' success in rehabilitating drug addicts, approached Malcolm X for his advice and assistance.

251. Sitkoff, Harvard. The Struggle for Black Equality, 1954-1980. NY: Hill and Wang, 1981. Malcolm X, pp. 127-128, 136, 152-155, 165, 185, 200-201, 205, 211-212.

The author argues that of all the Black leaders, Malcolm X seemed to understand the depth of the racial conflict of the 1960s; and only Malcolm appeared to view the Black struggle for equality as a power struggle, not a moral one. To virtually all Blacks, moreover, Malcolm X stood as an implacable symbol of resistance and champion of liberation.

252. Smith, Arthur. Rhetoric of Black Revolution. Boston, MA: Allyn and Bacon, 1969. Malcolm X, pp. 16-17, 50-55, 57, 60.

The writer suggests that Malcolm X was the great evangelist of Black unity, especially as he saw it manifested in Black nationalism... He concludes: "Only Malcolm X spoke from the real convictions and experiences of life; there was nothing theatrical or sophistic about his rhetoric."

253. ______________ and Stephen Robb, Editors. The Voice of Black Rhetoric: Selections. Boston, MA: Allyn and Bacon, 1971. Malcolm X, pp. 213-253.

Malcolm X's "The Ballot or the Bullet," "The Black Revolution," and "Prospects for Freedom," are included.

254. Smythe, Mabel M. The Black American Reference Book. Englewood Cliffs, NJ: Prentice-Hall, 1976. Malcolm X, pp. 84, 135-137, 395-397, 561-567, 610.

Author discusses him as a champion of oppressed, religious leader and founder of the Organization of Afro-American Unity.

255. Sobel, Lester A., Editor. Civil Rights: 1960-66. NY: Facts on File, Inc., 1967. Malcolm X (Malcolm Little), pp. 134, 167, 229, 230, 252, 283, 284, 285, 356 - 357, 457 - 458.

There are various discussions of Malcolm X's role in the Black Muslims and his impact on the Civil Rights Movement.

256. Spangler, Earl. The Blacks in America. Minneapolis, MN: Lerner Publications Co., 1980. Revised Edition. Malcolm X, p. 61.

Author states that Malcolm X was the Black Muslims most popular spokesman during the early 1960's and he attracted many urban Blacks to the Black Nationalist cause.

257. Staff of Black Star Publishing, Editors. The Political Thoughts of James Forman. Detroit, MI: Black Star Publishing, 1970. Malcolm X, pp. 43-44, 160, 177.

Mr. Forman states that after his rupture with Elijah Muhammad, who then advocated separation, Malcolm X took the road toward revolution and thereby began to galvanize the energies of many young Blacks reared in the northern ghettoes who were tired of the man's system.

258. Staples, Robert. Introduction to Black Sociology. NY: McGraw-Hill Book Company, 1976. Malcolm X, pp. 18, 164, 300, 302, 303, 305.

States that the Black student movement took many of the ideas of Malcolm X, such as self-determination, the need to study Black history and culture, and the necessity to have education related to the needs of the Black Community, and raised them as issues.

259. Steffgen, Kent H. The Bondage of the Free. Berkeley, CA: Vanguard Books, 1966. Malcolm X, pp. 39-42.

The writer suggests that before branching off on his own, Malcolm X was Elijah Muhammad's right hand man and in command of his "Fruit of Islam" peacekeeping guard which protects Elijah and maintains order throughout the establishment.

260. Sterling, Dorothy. Tear Down the Walls!: A History of the American Civil Rights Movement. NY: Doubleday & Company, Inc., 1968. Malcolm X, pp. 228-230.

Writer states that although the Black Muslims was headed by the Honorable Elijah Muhammad, their most effective spokesman was, for many years, a fiercely proud and brainy man who called himself Malcolm X. It was also surmised that in death Malcolm X became a legend- "Our black shining Prince"- whose influence spreads in widening circle from North ghettoes to the weather-beaten shanties of the South.

261. Storing, Herbert J. What Country Have I?: Political Writings by Black Americans. NY: St. Martin's Press, 1970. Malcolm X, pp. 145-163.

Author surmises that following a break with Elijah Muhammad in 1964, Malcolm entered into an extremely fruitful if often chaotic period during which he was principally concerned with thinking through his own position. This book also includes Malcolm's "The Ballot or the Bullet" speech.

262. Student Non-Violent Coordinating Committee. We Want Black Power. Chicago, IL: SNCC Office, 1967. (Leaflet).

One section is entitled, "What Brother Malcolm X Taught Us About Ourselves." Malcolm X taught Blacks that once a Black man discovers for himself a pride of his Blackness, he can throw off the shackles of mental slavery and become a MAN in the truest sense of the word.

263. Swan, L. Alex. Survival and Progress: The Afro-American Experience. Westport, CT: Greenwood Press, 1981. Malcolm X, pp. 45, 48, 51, 203, 210, 225.

The writer surmises that Malcolm X maintained that the so-called Black leaders in the United States were used by white liberals against the Black Revolution. According to Malcolm, the national Black leaders lost prestige and influence, and local leaders began to gain influence at the grass-root levels by stirring up these people, an accomplishment national leaders had not realized.

264. Synnestvedt, Sig. The White Response to Black Emancipation. NY: The Macmillan Company, 1972. Malcolm X, influence of, 200, 201, 202; advice to whites, 5; and Garveyism, 135; influence on students, 216, 217; and March on Washington, 197.

Various references are made to Malcolm X throughout this book.

265. Szasz, Thomas. Ceremonial Chemistry: The Ritual Persecution of Drugs, Addicts, and Pushers. Garden City, NY: Anchor Press, 1974. Malcolm X, pp. 82-96.

Chapter 7 is entitled "Drugs and Devils: The Conversion Cure of Malcolm X."

266. Taylor, Arnold H. Travail and Triumph: Black Life and Culture in the South Since the Civil War. Westport, CT: Greenwood Press, 1976. Malcolm X, p. 249.

The writer states that Malcolm X and other vocal leaders of the Black masses in the North who preached a philosophy of separatism or Black nationalism fed their disillusionment. Also surmises that Malcolm's assassination in 1965 transformed him into a martyr.

267. The Times News Teams. The Black Man in Search of Power: A Survey of the Black Revolution Across the World. London: Thomas Nelson and Sons, Ltd., 1968. Malcolm X, pp. 4, 67, 90, 91, 92, 102, 103, 144, 145, 160.

Malcolm X was quoted as saying: "I think the single worst mistake of the American Black organization, and their leaders, is that they have failed to establish direct brotherhood lines of communication between the independent nations of Africa and American Black people...."

268. Thomas, Tony, Editor. Black Liberation and Socialism. NY: Pathfinder Press, 1974. Malcolm X, pp. 84-91.

There is one section by Derrick Morrison, entitled, "Malcolm X and the Struggle for Independent Black Political Action." This article appeared in the March 17, 1972, issue of The Militant. The article outlines the pioneering role played by Malcolm X in initiating the drive for independent Black political action outside the two-party system. He also reviews attempts in this direction that have taken place since Malcom's death.

269. Thompson, Daniel C. Sociology of the Black Experience. Westport, CT: Greenwood Press, 1974. Malcolm X, pp. 148, 150-154.

The author observes that Malcolm X was one of the most charismatic Black leaders in history. He concludes: "He was much more than a Black Muslim preacher; he was a creative interpreter of the Black Experience...."

270. Thorpe, Earl E. Black Historians: A Critique. NY: William Morrow & Co., 1971. Malcolm X, p. 8.

States that Malcolm X and his mentor Elijah Muhammad "made each other."

271. Thum, Marcella. Exploring Black America: A History and Guide. NY: Athenum, 1975. Malcolm X, pp. 257, 359, 360, 371.

Author states that Malcolm X renamed himself El Hajj Malik El Shabazz after making a holy prigrimage to Mecca in 1964. Also states that he had become the greatest hero of modern times for many Black youths.

272. Toppins, Edgar A. A Biographical History of Blacks in America since 1528. NY: David McKay Co., 1971. Malcolm X, pp. 358-363.

A long biograhical sketch of Malcolm X is included in this collection.

273. Twombly, Robert C. Blacks in White America Since 1865: Issues and Interpretations. NY: David McKay Co., 1971.

Section 24 is entitled "Malcolm X, The Organization of Afro-American Unity (1965)." This is a position paper, by Malcolm X, on the Organization of Afro-American Unity.

274. United Federation of Teachers, AFL-CIO. Lesson Plans On Afro-American History. NY: United Federation of Teachers, AFL-CIO, 1969. Malcolm X, pp. 181-185.

The editors' aim for the user was "To learn about the life of Malcolm X."

275. Vincent, Theodore G. Black Power and The Garvey Movement. Berkeley, CA: Ramparts Press, 1971. Malcolm X, pp. 9, 22, 40, 136.

Author states that Malcolm X, whose father was a Garveyite, had a vision of the Black nation similar to that of Marcus Garvey. When asked about where the new nation would be, Malcolm was quoted as declaring: "It is right here, in the community, and in every Black community in America."

276. Vivian, C. T. Black Power and the American Myth. Philadelphia, PA: Fortress Press, 1970. Malcolm X, p. 96.

Author states that yet we persisted, for one thing was clear to us - the thing Malcolm X summed up in the phrase "The ballot or the bullet." It was clear that Black people had to become effective in the control of their own lives. Only the means to this control were in question, declares Mr. Vivian.

277. Wallace, Michele. Black Macho and the Superwoman. NY: Dial Press, 1978. Malcolm X, pp. 34, 36-38, 46.

It was stated that Malcolm X was the supreme Black patriarch. But in 1965 Black men murdered Malcolm, and with him died the chance for a Black patriarchy. No Black man would ever fill Malcolm's shoes. Everyone knew it, concludes the writer.

278. Warren, Robert Penn. Who Speaks for the Negro? NY: Random House, 1965. Malcolm X (Little), pp. 21, 22, 23, 136n., 138, 152, 190, 191, 195, 196, 197, 219, 244, 245, 248, 249-267, 276, 291, 299, 322, 330, 377, 381, 401, 409, 421n.

Malcolm X gives his views on "The Police State," "Civil Rights Leaders," "Abraham Lincoln," "John F. Kennedy," "Franklin D. Roosevelt," "Eleanor Roosevelt," "Elijah Muhammad" and many other topics.

279. Washington, Joseph R. Jr. Black & White Power Subreption. Boston, MA: Beacon Press, 1969. Malcolm X, pp. 59, 65, 108, 121, 135, 197.

Author surmises that Malcolm X never really came into his own until he severed his relations with Elijah Muhammad.

280. Weisboro, Robert G. Bittersweet Encounter: The Afro-American and the American Jew. Westport, CT: Negro Universities Press, 1970. Malcolm X, pp. 18, 93-97, 109, 148, 152, 182.

States that Black Muslims views on Zionists and Jews were perhaps articulated best by the late Malcolm X.

281. ________________. Ebony Kinship: Africa, Africans and the Afro-Americans. Westport, CT: Greenwood Press, Inc., 1973. Malcolm X, pp. 140, 143, 168, 182, 196, 199, 200, 201; Garvey and Malcolm X, 81, 82; on Mau Mau, 186; Pan-Africanism of Malcolm X, 205, 206; on West African "Brothers,", 173, 206; Malcolm X University, 207.

Various references are made to Malcolm X throughout this work.

282. Weiss, Karel, Editor. Under the Mask: An Anthology About Prejudice in America. NY: Delacorte Press, 1972. Malcolm X, pp. 117-121.

Malcolm X's essays, "Nightmare" and "Homeboy," from his autobiography, are included in this collection.

283. Williams, Jamye Coleman and McDonald Williams, Editors. The Negro Speaks: The Rhetoric of Contemporary Black Leaders. NY: Noble and Noble, 1970. Malcolm X, pp. 243-259.

Malcolm X's "The Ballot or the Bullet" speech is included in this collection. There is also a short biographical sketch of Malcolm before his speech.

284. Williams, Joe. New People: Miscegenation and Mulattoes in the United States. NY: Free Press, 1980. Malcolm X, pp. n18, 118, 188, 208.

States that Malcolm X was once known as "Detroit Red."

285. Wilmore, Gayrand S. Black Religion and Black Radicalism. Garden City, NY: Doubleday & Co., 1972. Malcolm X, pp. 3, 184, 219, 227, 238, 250-261, 300; assassination of, 254; Autobiography, 251-252; and Martin Luther King, Jr., 257-261.

The author declares that the radical faiths of Malcolm and Martin coalesce in the opaque depths of a Black spirituality that is neither Protestant nor Catholic, Christian nor Islamic in its essence, but both comprehend, and transcend, these ways of believing in God by experiencing his real presence by becoming one with him in suffering, in struggle and in the celebration of the liberation of man.

286. ________________ and James H. Cone, Editors. Black Theology: A Documentary History, 1966-1979. Mary-Knoll, NY: Orbis Books, 1979. Malcolm X, pp. 38, 67, 68, 69, 252, 304, 335, 336, 337, 353, 469, 564.

Various references are made to Malcolm X throughout this collection.

287. Woodward, C. Vann. The Strange Career of Jim Crow. NY: Oxford University Press, 1974. Malcolm X, pp. 202, 203.

The author surmises that Malcolm X was beyond doubt the most powerful voice and easily the most impressive and brilliant leader of the nationalist revival of the 1960's.

288. Young, Henry J. Major Black Religious Leaders Since 1940. Nashville, TN: Abingdon Press, 1979. "Malcolm X (1925-1965): Black Nationalist, Minister of Islam," pp. 73-81.

Various references are made to Malcolm X throughout this work.

289. Young, Richard P., Editor. Roots of Rebellion: The Evolution of Black Politics and Protest Since World War II. NY: Harper & Row, Publishers, 1970. Malcolm X, pp. 347-389.

Malcolm X's "Message to the Grass Roots" and "Prospects for Freedom in 1965" are included in this work.

290. Zinn, Howard. SNCC: The New Abolitionists. Boston, MA: Beacon Press, 1964. Malcolm X, pp. 213, 222.

The author asserts that the calls by Malcolm X and others for Negroes to use self-defense, and even retaliation, against acts of violence by whites, have not found approval by the SNCC organization.

4.
Major Articles About Malcolm X

A Selected List

291. "A Separate Path to Equality: The Shift From Moderates to Militants," Life, Vol. 65, No. 24, December 13, 1963, pp. 82-83.

The writer declares the man who spoke most clearly to those who despaired was Malcolm X. Malcolm spoke to the Negro, not FOR them, and he told them "look what you can do for yourselves."

292. "A Visit From the FBI," Malcolm X: The Man and His Times, John Henrik Clarke, Editor, pp. 182-204.

The FBI visited Malcolm X on May 29, 1964. Before they arrived, Malcolm set up a tape recorder, under a couch. This is their conversation.

293. Abernathy, Ralph. "My Last Letter to Martin (Luther King, Jr.)," Ebony, Vol. 23, No. 9, July, 1968, pp. 59-66.

The leader delivered this as a eulogy to King. He told King not to forget Malcolm X. The pastor surmised: "Malcolm may not have believed what we believed and he may not have preached, but he was a child of God and he was concerned about the welfare of his people."

294. Adegbalola, Gaye Todd. "A Conversation with Martin and Malcolm," Black Collegian, Vol. 33, No. 1, January-February, 1978, pp. 4, 6, 8, 83.

This article is a conversation composed of quotes and excerpts taken from actual speeches and writings of both leaders. The leaders commented on a variety of issues.

295. "An Interview with Malcolm X (February 9, 1965): First Time in Print," Militant, February 20, 1967, p. 5.

This is the first time that the interview was printed. Malcolm X was interviewed over the telephone on February 9, 1965.

296. Ahmed, Muhammed (Max Stanford). "The Roots of Pan-African Revolution," Black Scholar, Vol. 3, No. 1, May, 1972, pp. 48-55.

The writer argues that Malcolm X is the transitional figure in the development of revolutionary Black nationalism.

297. "All Africa Was For Malcolm X," The Militant, April 5, 1965, p. 4.

This is an excerpt from John Lewis and Donald Harris' tour of African countries, and their opinions of Malcolm X.

298. Allen, Robert. "Malcolm X: 2/21/65," Village Voice, February 17, 1966, p. 5.

There is a discussion of Malcolm X's assassination. Several eyewitnesses give their accounts.

299. ____________. "Malcolm X's Fatal Challenge to White Capitalism," National Guardian, February 18, 1967, p. 5.

The writer argues that Malcolm X linked U. S. freedom of Blacks with African freedom from colonial rule. He concludes: "Throughout the country a new generation of militant black youths are turning to Malcolm X's life and work for inspiration and guidance. Their hope is to bring the revolt of the world's oppressed into the stronghold of the oppressor."

300. Balk, Alfred and Alex Haley. "Black Merchants of Hate: The Black Muslims," Saturday Evening Post, Vol. 236, No. 3, January 26, 1963, pp. 68-74.

The writers discuss the Black Muslims and the role that Malcolm X played in it.

301. "Bar Malcolm X From Muslims' Chi Convention: Muslim Head Is Silent," New York Amsterdam News, February 15, 1964, pp. 1, 2.

Malcolm X was not allowed to attend the Nation of Islam's convention that was held in Chicago. No reason was given for keeping him out.

302. Barnes, Elizabeth. "Black Power," Young Socialist, Vol. 9, No. 6, August-September, 1966, pp. 12-

The writer surmises that many of the concepts of Black Power are the ideas held and explained by Malcolm X and many of the supporters of Black Power have been strongly influenced by Malcolm.

303. __________. "Nationwide Tributes to Malcolm X," Militant, Vol. 32, No. 10, March 4, 1968, p. 1.

Author points out that on the third anniversary of the death of Malcolm X, his life and his ideas are becoming known and accepted by masses of people who even a year ago were not aware of his importance as one of the greatest revolutionaries of our time.

304. __________. "The Impact of Malcolm X: His Ideas Keep Spreading," Militant, March 6, 1967, p. 4.

The writer contends that the many books by and about Malcolm X have helped his philosophy to spread.

305. Barnes, Jack and Barry Sheppard. "Interview with Malcolm X," Young Socialist, Vol. 8, No. 3, March-April, 1965, pp. 2-5.

Malcolm X discusses a variety of topics with Barnes and Sheppard. Malcolm saw the outlook for the Negro struggle in 1965 as a "Bloody" one.

306. __________. "In Tribute To Malcolm X," Young Socialist, Vol. 8, No. 4, May-June, 1965, pp. 4-5.

This is an excerpt from a speech delivered by the author, National Chairman, Young Socialist Alliance, at a memorial meeting for Malcolm X held at the New York Militant Labor Forum on March 5, 1965. He concludes: "He (Malcolm X) was living proof for our generation of revolutionists that it can and will happen here...."

307. __________. "Malcolm X: Recollections of a Visit," The Militant, February 22, 1965, p. 3.

The writer discusses an interview that he had with Malcolm X in January, 1965. He comments on a number of remarks made by Malcolm X.

308. Bates, Eveline. "We'LL Never Be The Same," American Dialog, Vol. 1, No. 2, October-November, 1964, pp. 23, 25, 26.

Author declares that Malcolm X's hate and distrust of the white man is irrational, a politically useful paranoia...And below the smoothest, most tolerant surfaces of this American white society, there is much factual base to support Malcolm X's supposed delusion, concludes the writer.

309. "The Beatification of Malcolm X," Times, March 1, 1968, p. 16.

This article discusses various cities in the United States that commemorated the third anniversary of Malcolm X's assassination. Malcolm's supporters wanted his birthday to be a national holiday.

310. Benson, Thomas W. "Rhetoric and Autobiography: The Case of Malcolm X," Quarterly Journal of Speech, Vol. 60, No. 1, February, 1974, pp. 1-13.

The writer argues that the constituents of rhetorical action are illustrated with special force in The Autobiography of Malcolm X, which achieves a unique synthesis of selfhood and rhetorical instrumentality.

311. Bethune, Lebert. "Malcolm X in Europe," Malcolm X: The Man and His Times, John Henrik Clarke, Editor, pp. 226-234.

The writer asserts: "I believe that Malcolm X was influential in Europe because it was easier to identify with him than to sympathize with him. The most articulate Afro-American voices in Europe before him, with the exception of Garvey, engendered sympathy much more readily than identification or fear."

312. Black, Pearl. "Malcolm X Returns." Liberator, Vol. 5, No. 1, January, 1965, pp. 5-6.

This article discusses Malcolm X's speech at the Audubon Ballroom in New York City on November 29, 1964. He told the group, in part: "Let us take from this meeting a feeling of unity. If we pull together, we can make it. And I feel that our efforts can bear fruits only by our becoming involved with international as well as national affairs."

313. Boggs, James. "The Influence of Malcolm X on the Political Consciousness of Black Americans, " Malcolm X: The Man and His Times, John Henrik Clarke, Editor, pp. 50-55.

Mr. Boggs states: "Among Black revolutionaries today there is no doubt whatsoever that the CIA engineered his (Malcolm X's) murder because they recognized the grave threat to American Masternationship which this linkup involved. Malcolm was only the first to be killed for this reason...."

314. Booker, James. "Is Mecca Trip Changing Malcolm?," New York Amsterdam News, May 23, 1964, p. 1.

The writer implies that Malcolm X's pilgrimage to Mecca may have changed his views about the true philosophy of Islam.

315. ____________. "Malcolm X Visiting Senate; Hits Leaders," New York Amsterdam News, March 28, 1964, p. 1.

Malcolm X states he would visit the United States Senate to hear what Southern Dixiecrats were saying to defeat the Civil Rights bill.

316. ______________. "Malcolm X: 'Why I Quit And What I Plan Next' - His Resignation Stuns Muhammad," New York Amsterdam News, March 14, 1964, pp. 1, 51.

Malcolm X states why he quite the Nation of Islam. Elijah Muhammad was surprised at his resignation. Malcolm X said he would resign from the Nation of Islam, but remain a Muslim.

317. ______________. "Seek To Evict Malcolm X From Home In Queens: Papers Already Filed In Court," New York Amsterdam News, April 18, 1964, pp. 1, 2.

The Nation of Islam sought to remove Malcolm X from his home in Queens, New York. Since he was no longer a Black Muslim, the sect wanted him off of their property.

318. Boulware, Marcus H. "Minister Malcolm, Orator Profundo," Negro History Bulletin, Vol. 30, No. 7, November, 1967, pp. 12-14.

The writer asserts that Malcolm X's language was bold, fierce and strong, complementing a full round voice flowing melodiously in the atmospheric breeze. He concludes that while Martin Luther King, Jr. gives us poetry, Malcolm X gave us prose.

319. Breitman, George. "Going To the UN Can Help, But It's No Cure-All," Militant, May 25, 1964, p. 5.

It was stated that Malcolm said that the Negro people's demands would have to be taken to the United Nations because the government in America is controlled by the same forces that oppress the Negro.

320. ________________. "In Defense of Black Power," International Socialist Review, Vol. 28, No. 1, January-February, 1967, pp. 4-16.

Author points out that Malcolm X set out early in 1964 to build a mass movement of freedom, justice, and equality, but was killed before he could do more than expound some basic principles and offer a personal example of fearless independence.

321. ________________. "Malcolm X," Dissent, Vol. 12, No. 4, Autumn, 1965, pp. 516-517.

This is a letter to the editor of Dissent commenting on Irving Howe's article that appeared in the summer issue of that publication. He states that Howe only adds to the legend of Malcolm X as "cop-out." The editor also printed a reply by Mr. Howe and Jeremy Larner to Mr. Breitman's letter.

322. ________________. "Malcolm X Spurs Civil Rights Forces: His Stand Can Unite and Build Movement," The Militant, April 6, 1964, p. 3.

The writer discusses several distinctive features of the program of Malcolm X's new organization.

323. ________________. "Malcolm X: The Man and His Ideas," The Militant, March 22, 1965, p. 4; Part II, March 29, 1965, p. 5.

This was the full text of a speech delivered at the Friday Night Socialist Forum in Detroit on March 5, 1965.

324. ________________. "Malcolm X's Murder and The New York Police," The Militant, July 12, 1965, pp. 1, 3.

The writer discusses the role of the New York police in the murder of Malcolm X.

325. ________________. "More Questions on Malcolm X's Murder," The Militant, August 9, 1965, p. 2.

The writer discusses the role of the New York police in the murder of Malcolm X. He said the police agents didn't do anything to catch the men who shot Malcolm X down right in front of them.

326. ________________. "New Force Can Bring Major Rights Gains," The Militant, March 30, 1964, p. 3.

The writer states that the Negro Movement is at a cross-road and Malcolm may be the one to give it new solutions and methods. Also because Malcolm X is one of the most able leaders and talented propagandists in this country, White or Black, with prestige extending far beyond the Muslims, especially among young people, states the author.

327. ________________. "The Impact of Malcolm X," Young Socialist, Vol. 9, No. 4, March-April, 1966, pp. 5-8, 15-16.

This is the edited text of a talk given by Breitman on February 11, 1966, to a memorial meeting commemorating Malcolm X one year after he was assassinated.

328. ________________. "Why Isn't Daily Press Interested in Who Killed Malcolm X?," The Militant, August 23, 1965, p. 2.

The writer suggests the local newspapers were not doing enough to help find the "real" murderer (s) of Malcolm X.

329. "British Guiana Youth Salute Malcolm X As Heroic Fighter," The Militant, March 22, 1965, p. 6.

The youths called Malcolm a courageously honest and dynamic leader.

330. "Brother Malcolm: His Theme Now Is Violence." U. S. News, Vol. 56, No. 12, March 23, 1964, p. 19.

This article states that for the first time a Negro leader (Malcolm X) is openly trying to woo his race away from nonviolence. According to this article, Malcolm said: "The Negro is justified to take any steps at all to achieve his equality...There can be no revolution without bloodshed."

331. "Brother Malcolm and Sister Jane: A Study in Sexism," Know, Vol. 1, No. 5, September, 1976, pp. 6-7.

Article discusses Malcolm X's opinion of Black women.

332. Burns, W. Haywood. "The Black Muslims in America: A Reinterpretation," Race, Vol. 5, No. 1, July, 1963,pp. 26-37.

Author discusses Malcolm X's role in the Black Muslims.

333. Campbell, Finley S. "Voices of Thunder, Voices of Rage: A Symbolic Analysis of a Selection from Malcolm X's Speech, 'Message to the Grass Roots'," Speech Teacher, Vol. 19, No. 2, March, 1970, pp. 101-110.

The writer analyzes Malcolm X's "Grass Roots" speech and suggests that Malcolm insisted that the very nature of a Black revolutionary encounter involves the need for polarization....

334. Capouya, Emile. "A Brief Return From Mecca," Saturday Review, November 20, 1965.

Author discusses Malcolm X's trip to Mecca. He said that trip changed Malcolm's opinion of the Nation of Islam.

335. Carmicael, Stokely. "We Are All Africans," Black Scholar, Vol. 1, No. 7, May, 1970, pp. 15-19.

This was a speech that Mr. Carmicael delivered at the opening dedication ceremony of Malcolm X Liberation University in Durham, NC in October, 1969. He made numerous references to Malcolm X and quoted from him.

336. Clarke, John Henrik. "Malcolm X: The Man and His Times," Negro Digest, Vol. 18, No. 7, May, 1969, pp. 23-27, 60-65.

The writer concludes: "Though he came from the American ghetto and directed his message to the people in the American ghetto first of all, he also became, in his brief lifetime, a figure of world importance."

337. Clasby, Nancy. "The Autobiography of Malcolm X: A Mythic Paradigm," Journal of Black Studies, Vol. 5, No. 1, September, 1974, Malcolm X, pp. 18-34.

The writer analyzes Malcolm X's autobiography and concludes: "His life ended on the stage of the Audubon Ballroom in a hail of assassin's bullets. But his significance was just beginning as the American incarnation of the desperate men who are plucking a new humanity from the global whirlwind of violence."

338. Cleage, Albert Jr., and George Breitman. "Myths About Malcolm X: Two Views," International Socialist Review, Vol. 28, No. 5, September-October, 1967, Malcolm X, pp. 33-60.

Rev. Cleage gives his personal reflections on the significance of Malcolm X. Mr. Breitman also gives his personal assessment of Malcolm.

339. ________________. "Myths About Malcolm X," Malcolm X: The Man and His Times, John Henrik Clarke, Editor, Malcolm X, pp. 13-26.

The author points out that Malcolm X wanted Blacks to organize and work for power. Because until you get power, Malcolm X is just a memory, declares the writer.

340. ________________. "The Malcolm X Myth," Liberator, Vol. 7, No. 6, June, 1967, Malcolm X, pp. 4-7.

The author states that we should remember that Malcolm's last message was organization. He concludes: "We didn't get it and that is why he died! We didn't have organization enough to protect him."

341. Cleaver, Eldridge. "Culture and Revolution: Their Synthesis in Africa," Black Scholar, Vol. 3, No. 2, October, 1971, Malcolm X, pp. 33-39.

The writer states that Malcolm X, as far as Afro-America is concerned, is the father of revolutionary Black nationalism. He also points out that Malcolm achieved the historic tasks of connecting the Afro-American struggle for national liberation with the national liberation and revolutionary struggles of Africa.

342. ________________. "Letters from Prison: On Malcolm X," Ramparts, August, 1966, Malcolm X, pp. 15-26.

He comments on Malcolm X's death. The writer surmises: "...The truth which Malcolm uttered had vanquished the whole passle of so-called Negro leaders and spokesmen who trifle and compromise with truth in order to curry favor with the white power structure...."

343. ________________. "The Muslims' Decline," Ramparts, Vol. 5, No. 8, February, 1967, pp. 10, 51.

The writer, a former Muslim, asserts that one of the reasons for the decline of the Muslims in prisons was the split in the Nation of Islam that developed over the callous ouster and subsequent murder of Malcolm X, who was the universal hero of Black prisoners.

344. Cleaver, Kathleen. "On Eldridge Cleaver by Kathleen Cleaver," The Black Panther, August 9, 1969, p. 3.

The writer contends that her husband, Eldridge Cleaver, left the Black Muslims when Malcolm X was put out and he organized a political group called African-American History and Culture Class when he was in prison, to follow Malcolm X's teachings.

345. Coburn, Mark D. "America's Great Black Hope (Joe Louis-Max Schmeling Fight)," American Heritage, Vol. 29, No. 6, October-November, 1978, p. 88.

Malcolm X was quoted in this article as declaring: "All the Negroes in Lansing, like Negroes everywhere, went wildly happy with the greatest celebration of race pride our generation has ever known. Every Negro boy old enough to walk wanted to be the next Brown Bomber."

346. Cocks, Jay. "Historical Primer: Malcolm X," Time, Vol. 99, No. 24, June 12, 1972, p. 62.

Review of film of biography of Malcolm X. This documentary was produced by Arnold Perl and Marvin Worth under the auspices of Warner Brothers.

347. Crawford, Marc. "The Ominous Malcolm X Exits From The Muslims," Life, Vol. 56, No. 12, March 20, 1964, pp. 40-40A.

The writer discusses the reasons why Malcolm X quit the Black Muslims. Crawford mentions that Malcolm gave his opinion on a variety of topics: Army, Martin Luther King, Jr., Paying Taxes, Separatism, Americanism, March on Washington, Nonviolence, the South, and Police Brutality.

348. Cruse, Harold W. "Revolutionary Nationalism and the Afro-American," Studies for the Left, Vol. II, No. 3, 1962, pp. 60-65.

Mr. Cruse supports his beliefs on the similarities between the "Negro's plight" and that of the "American" worker. He analyzes Marxism in light of the Negro's place in the United States labor force, emphasizing the relationship between the Negro masses and the Negro bourgeoisie, and the "Power Elite" from above. He also discusses the role Malcolm X played in the Black Nationalist Movement.

349. Damarest, David P. Jr. "The Autobiography of Malcolm X: Beyond Didacticism," CLA Journal, Vol. 16, No. 2 December, 1972, pp. 179-187.

The writer asserts that Malcolm X's autobiography has all sorts of didactic advice and moral and political insight that may often be more applicable to Blacks than to whites. He concludes: "But, above all, the book will appeal to whites because of its literary achievement of showing the fullness of Malcolm as a man."

350. Davis, Ossie. "Anti-Semitism and Black Power," Freedomways, Vol. 7. No. 1, Winter, 1967, pp. 77-79.

The writer contends that the beauty of Malcolm was that he was intelligent enough to grow away from past errors, and to stretch out his hands towards TRUTH even if they shot him down for it. Malcolm X was a Black Nationalist in the true sense of the word, states Mr. Davis.

351. ____________. "Our Own Black Shining Prince," Liberator, Vol. 5, No. 4, April, 1965, p. 7.

This is the text of the eulogy to Malcolm X by Davis delivered at Faith Temple Church of God and Christ, February 27, 1965.

352. ____________. "Why I Eulogized Malcolm X," Negro Digest, Vol. 15, No. 4, February, 1966, pp. 64-66.

The writer declares that no matter how much he disagreed with Malcolm X, he never doubted that Malcolm, even when he was wrong, was always that rarest thing in the world among us Negroes: a true man.

353. "Death of A Desperado; Assassination of Malcolm X," Newsweek, Vol. 66, No. 10, March 8, 1965, pp. 24-25.

The writer discusses the assassination of Malcolm X. It was stated that Malcolm's assassination turned out to be one of his few entirely accurate prophecies.

354. Diamond, Stanley. "The Apostate Muslim," Dissent, Vol. 12, No. 2, Spring, 1965, pp. 193-197.

The writer discusses Malcolm X's break with the Black Muslims. He aruges that Malcolm X was killed for ideological reasons.

355. DuBois, Shirley Graham. "The Beginning, Not The End," Malcolm X: The Man and His Times, John Henrik Clarke, Editor, pp. 125-127.

Mrs. DuBois concludes: "...Malcolm has paid this price! And in the unanimous coming together of the Afro-American press one glimpses the beginning of Malcolm X's victory. He may well rest in peace! A Salaam Alaikum!"

356. Editorial. "Lesson of Malcolm X," Saturday Evening Post, Vol. 237, No. 31, September 12, 1964, p. 84.

In this Editorial the writer suggests that if Malcolm X were not a Negro, his autobiography would be little more than a journal of abnormal psychology. He concludes: "The lesson of Malcolm X, and the lesson of the Mississippi showdown at Atlantic City, is that 19 million Negro Americans, who are equally taxed in all respects, still do not get equal representation, politically or otherwise."

357. Editorial. "Malcolm X," New York Times, February 22, 1965, p. 20.

The Editor suggests that Malcolm X's death could touch off war of vengeance. He warned against it.

358. Editorial. "Malcolm X and Martin Luther King, Jr.: Violence Versus Non-Violence," Ebony, April, 1965, pp. 168-169.

The Editor concludes that Malcolm X did not inspire the love that Martin Luther King, Jr. seems to win from the masses, but he did have their respect and, in many ways, their blessings. He concludes: "Whatever his motives were, Malcolm accomplished something for the Negro masses-and they appreciated it."

359. Editorial. "Murder of Malcolm X Is A Cruel Blow to the Cause of Black Emancipation," The Militant, March 1, 1965, pp. 1, 4.

The Editor declares that Malcolm X was the most uncompromising, incorruptible and talented leader of this country's 22 million oppressed, deprived and insulted Black citizens....

360. Editorial. "The Split Between Malcolm X and Elijah Muhammed," Liberator, Vol. 4, No. 7, June, 1964, p. 8.

The Editor contends that the split between the two men was the result of a profound crisis not only within the Muslim ranks but within the entire Negro civil rights movement as a whole. He also suggests that by leaving the Muslims, Malcolm actually exchanged one movement's crisis for another inasmuch as the official civil rights movement was also in a crisis.

361. Edwards, Lee M. "Peking and Malcolm X," New Republic, Vol. 152, No. 16, April 17, 1965, p. 44.

This was a letter replying to the March 27th article in the journal on Malcolm X. He told the Editor that Malcolm would always occupy a place in the hearts of peoples of color, whether white Americans like it or not.

362. "Elijah Suspends Malcolm," New York Amsterdam News, December 7, 1963, pp. 1, 2.

Elijah Muhammad suspends Malcolm X for his remarks about the assassination of President John Kennedy.

363. Elmessiri, Abdelwahab M. "Islam as a Pastoral in the Life of Malcolm X," Malcolm X: The Man and His Times, John Henrik Clarke, Editor, pp. 69-78.

Mr. Elmessiri argues, in part: "...Malcolm embraced the communitarian ideal of social action. His life after his actual conversion to Islam testifies to this fact...."

364. "Emancipation II," America, Vol. 108, June 1, 1063, p. 79.

Article discusses Malcolm X and Martin Luther King, Jr. as Black leaders.

365. Epps, Archie. "The Theme of Exile in Malcolm X's Harvard Speeches," Harvard Journal of Negro Affairs, Vol. 2, No. 1, 1968, pp. 40-54.

Malcolm X spoke at Harvard University on three different occasions: March 24, 1961; March 18, 1964; and December 16, 1964. The Harvard speeches represent three somewhat distinct phases of Malcolm X's life.

366. Essien-Udom, Ruby M. and E. U. Essien-Udom. "Malcolm X: An International Man," Malcolm X: The Man and His Times, John Henrik Clarke, Editor, pp. 235-267.

The writers discuss Malcolm X's transformation from the national spokesman for the Nation of Islam to an international spokesman for peoples of color. They conclude: "Alone, or almost single-handedly, Malcolm sought to link the Afro-American liberation movement with the liberation movement of the Third World, or what he called the Black Revolution."

367. Flick, Hank. "A Question of Identity: Malcolm X's Use of Religious Themes as a Means for Developing a Black Identity," Negro Educational Review, Vol. 31, Nos. 3-4, July-October, 1980, pp. 140-155.

This article examines Malcolm X's use of the teachings of the Black Church as a means of providing Black Americans with a new referent. To Malcolm, Allah (or God), was Black.

368. __________. "Malcolm X and the Prison Walls of America," Negro Educational Review, Vol. 30, No. 1, January, 1979, pp. 21-31.

Writer observes that in recording the Black experience as a prison, Malcolm not only synthesized the experience into a clearly defined cognitive whole, but also presented such a whole in terms the Blacks could understand and clearly envision.

369. Franklin, Robert. "Black Muslim Demonstration Protests Police Prosecution," The Militant, February, 18, 1963, p. 1.

Malcolm X spoke to the demonstrators in New York and told them, in part: "In Times Square Negroes will expose the hypocrisy of American 'democracy'."

370. Gardner, Jigs. "The Murder of Malcolm X," Monthly Review, Vol 16, No. 12, April, 1965, pp. 802-805.

The writer suggests that Malcolm's assassination was a profoundly political event. He was murdered because of his ideas and his politics. He represented a threat to the privileges and vested interests of powerful groups, both white and Black.

371. Garnett, Jay. "Tribute Paid to Malcolm X," The Militant, March 8, 1965, p. 8.

This tribute was paid to him in Detroit by his friends and supporters. Henry King said: "Malcolm X was the conscience of the Negro people."

372. Geevskii, I. A. and S. A. Chervonnaia. "Mal'Kil'M Iks" (Malcolm X), Novaia i Noveishais Istoria (Russia), Vol. 2, 1972, pp. 92-108.

The authors give an overview of Malcolm X's life. They point out how and why he became a Black Muslim.

373. Gillespie, Marcia A. "Getting Down," Essence, Vol. 3, No. 1, May, 1972, pp. 39-41.

The Editor asserts that Malcolm's philosophy of life, a never-ending demand that we cease begging, beseeching and existing like slaves, and start living in dignity as we are supposed to, continues to burn in our hearts and minds.

374. Glanville, Brian. "Malcolm X," New Statesman, Vol. 67, No. 1735, June 21, 1964, pp. 901-902.

Malcolm X comments on a variety of topics: "Black Muslims," "Manhood," "Racism," "Violence," "Non-violence," etc.

375. Grant, Earl. "The Last Days of Malcolm X," Malcolm X: The Man and His Times, John Henrik Clarke, Editor, pp. 83-113.

The writer, a close friend of Malcolm X, discusses the last terrible thirteen days in Malcolm X's life.

376. Griffin, John Howard. "Ten Years Later: The Legend Grows: The Unsolved Mystery Murder of Malcolm X," Sepia, Vol. 24, No. 2, February, 1975, pp. 18-26.

The writer cites new findings and traces the remarkable transformation in attitudes about Malcolm X...once viewed as a dangerous hate monger by Blacks and whites alike during his lifetime. Today (1975) Malcolm has gradually come to be regarded as a kind of saint who went to his martyrdom under a hail of bullets in a Harlem meeting hall.

377. Haley, Alex. "Playboy Interview: Malcolm X," Playboy, Vol. 10, May, 1963, pp. 53-54.

Malcolm discussed a variety of issues: race problems in America, Nation of Islam and Black Muslims, and the future of Blacks in the United States.

378. Hall, Gwendolyn Midlo. "St. Malcolm and the Black Revolutionist," Negro Digest, Vol. 17, No. 1, November, 1967, pp. 4-11.

Miss Hall observes that because the Black revolutionist has not learned enough from the life of Malcolm, he tends to become a cultist offering ritualistic compensation for blackness, and/or a poseur, playing the role of spokesman of the Black masses for the benefit of those white folks who don't know any better. She surmises: "A revolution in the psyche of one man can become an all-powerful force for social change. St. Malcolm was such a man."

379. Hamilton, Bobb. "El Hajj Malik Shabazz: Leader, Prophet, Martyr," Soulbook, Vol. 1, No. 2, Spring, 1965, pp. 81-84.

The author concludes: "...They think they buried Malcolm; they buried a husk. He lives, He breathes! He walks and talks twenty-five million strong! Look for us in the whirlwind!"

380. Handler, M. S. "Malcolm Rejects Racist Doctrine: Also Denounces Elijah (Muhammad) as a Religious 'Faker'," New York Times, October 4, 1964, p. 59.

381. ____________. "Malcolm X Sees Rise in Violence; Says Negroes Are Ready to Act in Self-Defense," New York Times, March 13, 1964, p. 20.

382. ____________. "Malcolm X Splits with Muhammad: Suspended Muslim Leader Plans Black Nationalist Political Movement," New York Times, March 9, 1964, p. 42.

Malcolm X states he would form a different organization that would help Blacks politically and economically.

383. Hansen, Joseph. "Rowan's Smear of Malcolm X," The Militant, March 15, 1965, p. 4.

This editorial comments on Carl T. Rowan's smear of Malcolm X. Mr. Rowan was then (1965) Director of the United States Information Agency.

384. Harding, Vincent. "The Black Wedge in America: Struggle, Crisis and Hope, 1955-1975," Black Scholar, Vol. 7, No. 4, December, 1975, pp. 28-30, 35-46.

The author mentions the role Malcolm X played in the Black struggle for equality.

385. Harper, Frederick D. "A Reconstruction of Malcolm X's Personality," Afro-American Studies, Vol. 3, No. 1, June, 1972, pp. 1-6.

The writer concludes that Malcolm X possessed several significant personality traits which helped him to attain a position of visibility and leadership. Professor Harper also analyzes his most salient personality characteristic, and identified some of his weaknesses.

386. ____________________. "The Influence of Malcolm X on Black Militancy," Journal of Black Studies, Vol. 1, No. 4, June, 1971, pp. 387-402.

The writer argues that the personality and philosophy of Malcolm X strongly influenced the life and philosophy of Eldridge Cleaver, Black militant leaders, and Black militant students.

387. Hatch, Roger D. "Racism and Religion: The Contrasting Views of Benjamin Mays, Malcolm X, and Martin Luther King, Jr.," Journal of Religious Thought, Vol. 20, Winter, 1980, pp. 26-36.

The writer discusses Malcolm X's religious views and how it differed from other civil rights leaders' philosophy.

388. Henry, Lawrence and Richard Henry. "Malcolm X," Now, March-April, 1966.

The writers comment on Malcolm X's impact on Black people in the United States.

389. ________________. "Malcolm X Lives," Cavalier, June, 1966.

Author discusses Malcolm X's role in the civil rights struggle.

390. Henry, Milton. "New Glory Visits Malcolm X," Now (Detroit), March-April, 1966.

The writer states that Malcolm X was in essence an evangelist-not an organizer. He also concludes Malcolm expected to be killed, and resigned himself and family to such a possibility.

391. Hentoff, Nat. "Elijah in the Wilderness," Reporter, Vol. 23, August 4, 1960, pp. 37-40; September 29, 1960, p. 10.

The writer discusses Malcolm X's role in the Nation of Islam.

392. Herman, David. "Black Revolt in Los Angeles," Young Socialist, Vol. 9, No. 1, September-October, 1965, p. 6.

Writer states that of all the public figures who had spoken about the Black revolt or "Negro revolution" in America, only Malcolm X predicted what was coming, explained it clearly, and supported without reservation any action Afro-Americans would take to win freedom, justice, and equality.

393. ______________. "Cheering Harlem Rally Hears Malcolm X Rip U. S. Racism," The Militant, June 15, 1964, pp. 1, 3.

Malcolm X told the crowd, in part: "The capitalistic system cannot produce freedom for the Black man. Slavery produced this system and this system can only produce slavery...."

394. ______________. "Harlem Rally Demands: 'Hands Off the Congo!, Says Malcolm X and Others'," The Militant, December, 21, 1964, pp. 1, 2.

Malcolm X spoke to about 1,500 people and told them that Tshombe was "the worst African ever born."

395. ______________. "Malcolm X Announces Rally to Launch New Organization," The Militant, June 29, 1964, p. 1.

Malcolm X spoke at the Audubon Ballroom and told the crowd in part: "...We need an organization that no one downtown can dictate to...that no one downtown loves. Not only individuals, but other organizations will be able to join as long as they endorse the motto: 'by any means necessary'."

396. ______________. "Malcolm X Assails U. S. Role in Congo," The Militant, December 7, 1964, pp. 1, 3.

At a press conference held upon his arrival, Malcolm X declared in part: "...We want the world to know we don't like what Sam (U. S. Government) is doing to our Brothers in the Congo."

397. ______________. "Malcolm X at Militant Labor Forum," The Militant, January 18, 1965, p. 2.

Author comments on Malcolm X's various speeches at the monthly meeting of the Militant Labor Forum. This organization supported Malcolm when he broke with the Black Muslims.

398. ______________. "Malcolm X Back from Africa-Urges Black United Front," The Militant, June 1, 1964, p. 8.

Malcolm observed that on his trip to the Mideast and Africa he had lined up support in the countries he visited for bringing charges in the United Nations that human rights of the Negro people in the U. S. were being denied.

399. ______________. "Malcolm X Details Black Nationalist Views," The Militant, April 20, 1964, p. 8.

All 600 people heard Malcolm X speak at Palm Gardens in Harlem. He asserts, in part: "The whites can help if they're progressive-minded, but my observation and analysis of the type of help that they've been giving makes me very cautious about the help they offer...."

400. ______________. "Malcolm X Discusses Bombing of Home," The Militant, February 22, 1965, p. 1.

He charged that the bombing of his home had been ordered by Elijah Muhammad. Malcolm X also asserted that the Black Muslims had become "a criminal organization in the hands of a man who's senile."

401. ______________. "Malcolm X Launches a New Organization," The Militant, July 13, 1964, p. 1.

Malcolm X called his new organization "The Organization of Afro-American Unity." He also gave a statement of its goals and objectives.

402. ______________. "Malcolm X's Last Meeting," The Militant, February 22, 1965, pp. 1, 2.

The writer discusses the last meeting that Malcolm X attended of the Organization of Afro-American Unity.

403. ______________. "Malcolm X to Organize Mass Voter Registration," The Militant, April 6, 1964, pp. 1, 3.

Malcolm X states that the first campaign of his new Black nationalist movement would be a massive voter-registration drive. Malcolm also declares: "...If we aren't wanted we should go back home. Our homeland is the continent of Africa...."

404. ______________. "Reviews and Reports," The Militant, May 24, 1965, p. 4.

The author surveyed a number of pamphlets and articles that had been published since Malcolm X's death.

405. ______________. "3000 Cheer Malcolm X at Opening Rally in Harlem," The Militant, March 30, 1964, p. 1.

At this rally at the Rockland Palace in Harlem, Malcolm X told the group, in part: "...If the government won't find out who bombed the church in Birmingham...then we'd better do something...."

406. Holt, Len. "Malcolm X the Mirror," Liberation, Vol. 6, No. 2, February, 1966, pp. 4, 5.

Mr. Holt argues that how advantageously Black people use the Malcolm legacy will be shaped on how well they knew Malcolm's objectives.

407. Howe, Irving. "New Styles in 'Leftism'," Dissent, Vol. 12, No. 3, Summer, 1965, pp. 295-322.

The writer concludes, in part: "...For Malcolm, intransigent in words and nihilistic in reality, never invoked the possibility or temptations of immediate struggle; he never posed the problems, confusions and risks of maneuver, compromise, retreat. Brilliantly Malcolm spoke for a rejection so complete it transformed him into an apolitical spectator, or in the language his admirers are more inclined to use than I am, a pure 'cop-out'."

408. Hoyt, Charles A. "The Five Faces of Malcolm X," Negro American Literature Forum, Vol. 4, No. 4, Winter, 1970, pp. 107-112.

The author discusses the five revolutions of Malcolm X's life: 1. Malcolm Little, 2. Detroit Red, 3. Satan, 4. Malcolm X, 5. El Hajj Malik El-Shabazz.

409. Hunt, Frank. "Malcolm X Still Lives," Baltimore Afro-America, February 19, 1966.

The author argues that although Malcolm X is dead, his philosophy still lives on.

410. Ihde, Horst. "Die Black Muslims in Den USA (The Black Muslims in the USA), Wissenchaftliche Zeitschrift der Humboldt-Universitat Berlin (East Germany), Vol. 7, No. 5, 1968, pp. 689-701.

The writer suggests that Malcolm X's philosophy was influenced by Marcus Garvey. He also discusses the role Malcolm played in the Black Muslims.

411. Illo, John. "The Rhetoric of Malcolm X," Columbia University Forum, Spring, 1966, pp. 5-12.

The writer argues that the rhetoric of Malcolm X was in the perennial traditions of the art, but appropriate to his audiences and purpose-perennial because appropriate. Mr. Illo also surmises that though he may be diluted, or obliterated, or forgotten by the established civil rights movement, which is built into the consensus, Malcolm was for all times an artist and thinker.

412. "Is Malcolm X Clueing in Africans on U. S.?," The Militant, January 11, 1965, p. 8.

This article comments on Malcolm X's trip to Africa and what he told Africans when he visited there.

413. Jackson, James E. "A Fighting People Forging New Unity," The Worker, July 7, 1963. Also appears in Political Affairs, August, 1963, under the title, "A Fighting People Forging Unity."

The writer concludes: "...Malcolm X and his fellow cultist leaders work untiringly to undermine the prestige of such vital leaders as the Rev. Martin Luther King, Roy Wilkins and others...."

414. Johnson, John H. "Violence Versus Nonviolence," Ebony, Vol. 20, No. 6, April, 1965, pp. 168-169.

Editorial compares Malcolm X's methods with Martin Luther King, Jr.'s method of achieving racial equality. Editor states that Malcolm X did not inspire the love that King seems to win from the masses, but he did have their respect and, in many ways, their blessings. Whatever his motives were, Malcolm accomplished something for the Negro masses--and they appreciated it.

415. Kahn, Tom and Bayard Rustin. "The Ambiguous Legacy of Malcolm X," Dissent, Vol. 12, No. 2, Spring, 1965, pp. 188-192.

The writers argue, in part: "Malcolm X was a child of the ghetto and he was dedicated to the preservation of the ghetto, which he thought could be either transformed from within or transplanted to a happier environment. That was his central error, and he cannot be easily forgiven it. Every prostitute or dope addict he and the Muslims claimed to reform, the ghetto replaced many times over. The moral transformation he advocated could never take place, because there is a limit to what the will can alone achieve...."

416. Kaminsky, Marc. "Radical Affirmatives," American Scholar, Vol. 36, Autumn, 1967, pp. 621-630.

A discussion of Malcolm X's autobiography is included in this article.

417. Karenga, Maulana. "Malcolm and the Messenger: Beyond Psychological Assumptions to Political Analysis," Blacknews, Vol. 4, No. 21, 1982, pp. 4-11.

Karenga concludes: "Whatever religious role and status Malcolm and Muhammad had (and they were of great significance), they both also had a political role and status and thus, their conflict was shaped by politics as much as, if not more than, religion."

418. ________________. "The Socio-Political Philosophy of Malcolm X," Western Journal of Black Studies, Vol. 3, No. 4, Winter, 1979, pp. 251-262.

The writer survey's Malcolm X's life. He argues that at the core of his social and political thought is the fundamental concept of Black nationalism.

419. Kelley, William Melvin. "On Racism, Exploitation and the White Liberal," Negro Digest, Vol. 16, No. 3, January, 1967, pp. 5-12.

The author asserts that if Malcolm X had lived he would have taught us that even before we can discover what other people did about their problems, we must first be certain we know the true nature of our own problems. He concludes: "It would be a great shame,..., if we moved backwards from the point to which at times very much against our will, he had pushed us."

420. Kendrick, Curtis. "On The Autobiography of Malcolm X," Journal of the National Medical Association, Vol. 63, No. 1, January, 1971, pp. 43-49, 79.

The writer discusses how this autobiography explains Malcolm X's life and the dynamics of his character development. He also drew some comparison with the Apostle Paul, his personality, conversion, subsequent apostolic influence and the manner in which he faced an untimely death by violent means.

421. Kerina, Mburumba. "Malcolm X: The Apostle of Defiance-An African View," Malcolm X: The Man and His Times, John Henrik Clarke, Editor, pp. 114-119.

The writer suggests that though Malcolm did not live to witness the materialization of his dreams, the seeds that he planted have started to germinate. He concludes, in part: "...Black men and women in Africa, America, and England are now waging their last struggle for total emancipation and the reconstruction of the societies in which they currently live...."

422. Kgositsile, William Keorapetse. "Brother Malcolm and the Black Revolution," Negro Digest, Vol. 18, No. 1, November, 1968, pp. 4-10.

Mr. Kgositsile, an exile from South Africa, declares: "Brother Malcolm was our Dream, our Promise, our Hope, a concrete vector of our desire and possibility, the actual emobdiment of what we strive to be-intrepid, righteous, dedicated to the destruction of evil, dedicated to the rebuilding of Man and our possibilities as only the sincere lover can be constantly moving."

423. ______________________________. "Malcolm X and the Black Revolution: The Tragedy of a Dream Deferred," Malcolm X: The Man and His Times, John Henrik Clarke, Editor, pp. 42-49.

The author surmises, in part: "The recurrence of Malcolm's spirit is the source of our power, the power of the best possible productive uses of our lives...."

424. Knebel, Fletcher. "A Visit With the Widow of Malcolm X," Look, Vol. 33, No. 5, March 4, 1969, pp. 74-77, 79, 80.

Malcolm X's widow comments on a variety of topics. She declares: "Maclolm didn't hate whites. He hated what whites had done to blacks."

425. Lacy, Leslie Alexander. "Malcolm X in Ghana," Malcolm X: The Man and His Times, John Henrik Clarke, Editor, pp. 217-225.

The writer states that Malcolm X admired Kwame Nkrumah, President of Ghana, for his militant policies and his strong advocacy of Black solidarity.

426. Lerner, Max. "Malcolm X and 'White Devils'," Detroit News, March 16, 1964.

Author comments on Malcolm X's opinion of white people.

427. Les, Payne. "An Interview With Malcolm X," Encore, Vol. 2, No. 5, May, 1973, pp. 52-56.

The author holds an imaginary, but real, conversation with the fallen leader. All quotes attributed to Malcolm X were taken from interviews and speeches that he made during his lifetime.

428. Lester, Julius. "The Angry Children of Malcolm X," Sing Out, November, 1966.

The writer suggests that more than any other person Malcolm X was responsible for the new militancy that entered the movement in 1965.

429. Lewis, Raymond. "Malcolm X Was a Black Man," The Black Panther, May 19, 1970, pp. 10-11.

The writer suggests that it's the thoughts of Huey P. Newton, underscored by the ideology and philosophy seeded by Malcolm X, that holds the Black Panther Party together and constitutes its foundation....

430. Lincoln, C. Eric. "Meaning of Malcolm X," Christian Century, Vol. 82, No. 14, April 7, 1965, pp. 431-433.

The author surmises that it does not promote the cause of responsible leadership to deny the importance of Malcolm X to the particular segment of people whose political and/or ideological leader he was, or sought to be; to do so is to deny by implication the threat he represented to the tranquility and effectiveness of the more sophisticated procedures advanced by more acceptable leaders.

431. ________. "Meaning of Malcolm X," Malcolm X: The Man and His Times, John Henrik Clarke, Editor, pp. 7-12.

The writer concludes that Malcolm X was a remarkably gifted and charismatic leader whose hostility and resentment symbolized the dreadful stamp of the Black ghetto...a man whose philosophies of racial determination and whose pragmatic comments made him unacceptable as a participant in peaceful social change....

432. Lubell, Samuel. "Did Malcolm's Ironic Role Advance Rights?," Detroit Free Press, March 1, 1965.

Author states that Malcolm X had a positive impact on Blacks' civil rights struggle in the United States.

433. Lynch, Acklyn. "America: The Meaning of Malcolm X," Black Collegian, Vol. 35, No. 4, December, 1980, pp. 38-40.

The writer discusses the impact that Malcolm X had on the Black struggle in America.

434. Macinnes, Colin. "Malcolm, The Lost Hero," Negro Digest, Vol. 16, No. 7, May, 1967, pp. 4-5.

This article was reprinted from The London Sunday Times. Colin gives a Briton's viewpoint. He surmises: "... But his example and influence are germinal. For the prime American problem-and perhaps world problem-is the racial one."

435. Major, Clarence. "Malcolm X the Martyr," Vol. 22, Negro Digest, Vol. 15, No. 2, December, 1966, pp. 37-42.

The writer gives a personal memoir of Malcolm X and discusses various aspects of his life. He concludes: "The only thing we are sure of is that this is a time of challenge, and that Malcolm X had a very real part of it."

436. "Malcolm and His Changes," Sacramento Observer, May 20, 1971, p. A-8.

This article suggests that Malcolm X was simultaneously broadening his horizons and zeroing in on American imperialism-this product of the segregated, locked-in ghetto who broke through and over the walls of national boundary and race to become an internationalist.

437. "Malcolm X Addresses Black Muslim 'Unity Meeting' in Harlem, NYC," New York Times, August 11, 1963, p. 1.

438. "Malcolm X Bids Africans Take Negro Issue to U.N.," New York Times, July 18, 1964, p. 2.

Malcolm X urged African leaders to take up the cause of civil rights before the United Nations.

439. "Malcolm X: Black Revolution Is Part of World-Wide Struggle," The Militant, April 27, 1964.

Speech he delivered to the Militant Labor Forum at New York's Palm Gardens Ballroom on April 8, 1964.

440. "Malcolm X Denounces Use of Children; Criticizes Rev. King Campaign as 'Exercise in Futility and Erroneous Approach to Problems of Race Relations'; Says Majority of Demonstrators Refused to Accept King's Doctrine of Nonviolence," New York Times, May 11, 1963, p. 9.

Malcolm X did not believe that children should be used in civil rights demonstrations.

441. "Malcolm X Film on (WABC-TV) 'Like It Is'," New York Amsterdam News, February 25, 1978, p. D-7.

Gil Noble, who wrote, produced and narrated the film, states that since his death, the man's image has taken on a new meaning. Members of both the Black and White communities are recognizing the importance behind his life and death, states Noble.

442. "Malcolm X Hits Both Goldwater and Johnson," The Militant, September 14, 1964, p. 8.

Malcolm declares that both Goldwater and Johnson are about the same and he would vote for neither.

443. "Malcolm X in Cairo Urges African Aid to U. S. Negroes," The Militant, August 24, 1964, p. 1.

This is an excerpt from a speech Malcolm X made on July 17th before the Organization of African Unity in Cairo, Egypt.

444. "Malcolm X Makes Pilgrimage to Mecca; Describes New Insights on Race Relations," New York Times, May 8, 1964, p. 1.

Malcolm X suggests that he has a different outlook on white people after making a pilgrimage to Mecca.

445. "Malcolm X of Black Muslims Criticizes Rev. Dr. King Approach to Race Relations; Says White Southerners Are More Forthright in Opposing Desegregation Than 'Hypocritical' Liberal Whites in North," New York Times, May 11, 1963, p. 9.

446. "Malcolm X on Vietnam War," Young Socialist, Vol. 10, No. 4, May, 1967, p. 16.

These are quotations selected from Malcolm X Speaks that show how his opposition to the Vietnam War was part of his overall revolutionary outlook.

447. "Malcolm X Predicted Outbreaks Inevitable," The Militant, August 23, 1965, p. 1.

Before his death, Malcolm X predicted social explosions in the Black ghettos of America like the one in Los Angeles.

448. "Malcolm X Repeats Call for Negro Unity on Rights," New York Times, June 29, 1964.

Malcolm urged all Blacks to work together for the cause of civil and human rights.

449. "Malcolm X Replies to Mayor Yorty Attack on Muslim Movement," New York Times, July 27, 1962, p. 8.

Malcolm states that the Black Muslims would defend themselves if they are attacked by others.

450. "(Malcolm X) Says He Is Now World Muslim League Representative with Authority to Open Muslim Center in New York City," New York Times, October 11, 1964, p. 48.

After Malcolm returned from Mecca, he declared that he would represent the World Muslim League in the United States.

451. "Malcolm X Scorns Rev. M. L. King's Nonviolence Policy," New York Times, June 5, 1963, p. 29.

Malcolm X observes that Dr. King's policy of nonviolence was ineffective and Blacks should not turn the other cheek.

452. "Malcolm X Sees End of Muslims," Washington Sunday Star, August 30, 1964.

Malcolm X states that the Nation of Islam must change its philosophy.

453. "Malcolm X Slain: Vendetta by Rivals Feared," Senior Scholastic, Vol. 86, No. 6, March 11, 1965, p. 21.

This article discusses Malcolm X's assassination and rivalry between Malcolm X's Organization for Afro-American Unity and the Nation of Islam. On the murder, Martin Luther King, Jr. asserts: "This vicious assassination should cause our whole society to see that violence and hatred are evil forces that must be cast into unending limbo."

454. "Malcolm X Talks with Kenneth B. Clark," Malcolm X: The Man and His Times, John Henrik Clarke, Editor, pp. 168-181.

Prof. Clark interviewed Malcolm in June, 1963. They discussed a variety of topics: Malcolm X's childhood, Ku Klux Klan, Prison, Black Muslims, Martin Luther King, Jr., NAACP, etc.

455. "Malcolm X Tells of Death Threat," New York Amsterdam News, March 21, 1964, p. 1.

Malcolm X told police that he received a death threat.

456. "Malcolm X to Reveal New Plans," New York Amsterdam News, February 13, 1965, p. 5.

Malcolm X states that he would form a new political organization that would be different from other Black organizations in the United States.

457. "Malcolm X Urges American Negroes to Look to Africa 'Culturally, Philosophically and Spiritually', Charges USIA Seeks to Present Idyllic Picture of American Negro to Africans," New York Times, December 13, 1964, p. 80.

Malcolm X observes that Black Americans should remember that Africa is their motherland and should support the continent.

458. "Malcolm X Urges 'United Black Front'," New York Times, August 11, 1963, p. 1.

Malcolm suggests that all Black people should work together in order to better conditions of Blacks in the United States.

459. "Malcolm X Will Distribute 35 Scholarships," The Militant, November 2, 1964, p. 8.

Malcolm X announced that he received a number of scholarships from African and Arab countries which would enable young Afro-Americans to go abroad to study - expense free.

460. "Malcolm X Woos Two Rights Leaders (Bayard Rustin and Rev. Milton A. Galamison); Asks 'Forgiveness' for Past Remarks and Seeks Unity," New York Times, May 19, 1964, p. 22.

Malcolm X surmises that in the future he would seek the aid and support of other Black leaders.

461. Mandel, John. "The Didactic Achievement of Malcolm X's Autobiography," Afro-American Studies, March, 1972.

The writer discusses the impact that Malcolm X's autobiography has had on Black political thought in the United States.

462. Massaquoi, H. J. "Mystery of Malcolm X," Ebony, Vol. 19, No. 11, September, 1964, pp. 38-46.

It was observed that until put to a real test, the true intentions of Malcolm X - like the man himself - will remain shrouded in speculation and mystery. He concluded: "Only one thing is clear: neither the Black Muslim movement without him, nor the right movement with him, will ever be the same."

463. Mayfield, Julian. "Profile: Malcolm X: 1925-1965," African Review, Vol. 1, No. 1, May, 1965, p. 9.

Mr. Mayfield asserts/concludes, in part: "What is certain is that the sons and daughters of Africa in the Western world have suffered a major set-back, for Malcolm was the only national leader who spoke the language of the dispossessed masses, the only one who had a chance and the will to galvanize them into revolutionary activity...."

464. "Militant: St. Malcolm X," Newsweek, Vol. 73, No. 9, March 3, 1969, pp. 27-28.

The author declares that Malcolm X, four years dead, is at the height of his power. It was also pointed out that the Malcolm explosion remains no less real-and its breadth and depth would have surprised Malcolm himself.

465. Montgomery, Paul L. "Malcolm X Exhorts Negroes to Look to African Culture," New York Times, December 13, 1964, p. 202.

Malcolm X encouraged Black Americans to look to Africa for their cultural roots.

466. Moon, Henry Lee. "The Enigma of Malcolm X," Ebony, Vol. 72, No. 4, April, 1965, pp. 226-227.

The writer concludes: "In light of today's (1965) developments Malcolm was an anachronism-vivid and articulate but, nevertheless, divorced from the mainstream of Negro American thoughts."

467. Moore, Louise. "When a Black Man Stood Up," Liberator, Vol. 6, No. 7, July, 1966, pp. 7-9.

Author states that no one could remain the same after the brutal slaying of our beloved Malcolm. She suggests, to us Black people, Malcolm was everything that we could someday become.

468. Morrison, Allan. "Who Killed Malcolm X," Ebony, Vol.20, No. 12, October, 1965, pp. 135-142.

The writer asserts that unless most of the questions surrounding Malcolm's death can be answered, many knowledgeable persons will refuse to accept as conclusive a guilty verdict against any one, or all the three suspects, barring unequivocal confessions. He concludes: "Whatever the outcome of the upcoming trial, theories regarding motives for the murder are likely to proliferate for years as will the legend that is now in the making about the man called Malcolm X."

469. Morgan, John. "Malcolm X's Murder," New Statesman, Vol. 69, No. 1772, February 16, 1965, p. 310.

The writer declares that Malcolm X did not believe in separatism. He said Malcolm's attitude was moving closer and closer to Martin Luther King's. Together they would have been a formidable force, concludes Morgan.

470. Moses, Wilson J. "A Reappraisal of the Garvey Movement," Black Scholar, Vol. 4, No. 3, November-December, 1972, pp. 38-49.

Author asserts that modern day Black nationalism must be in the spirit of Malcolm X.

471. "Mrs. Malcolm X," Newsweek, Vol. 74, No. 18, November 3, 1969, p. 16.

Writer gives a brief assessment of Mrs. Betty Shabazz's current activities. Malcolm X's widow states: "Malcolm always said it was just as noble for Black people to fight for their human rights as it is for an Irishman, a Jew, a Russian, an Arab, or a Chinese."

472. "Murder of Malcolm X," Black Flag, No. 6, April 29, 1965, pp. 7-8.

It was pointed out that the murder of Malcolm X led to a tide of fury everywhere.

473. "My Next Move!-Malcolm X: An Exclusive Interview," New York Amsterdam News, May 30, 1964, pp. 1, 52.

474. Nadle, Marlene. "Malcolm X: The Complexity of a Man in the Jungle," Village Voice, February 25, 1965.

In this article Malcolm tells why he sometimes gave sensational answers to reporters that interviewed him. He suggests that if they had asked probing, intelligent questions, they would have gotten different answers.

475. Neal, Lawrence P. "A Reply to Bayard Rustin-The Internal Revolution," Liberator, Vol. 5, No. 7, July, 1965, pp. 6-7.

The author states that Bayard Rustin had no right to criticize Malcolm X and he should not be allowed to speak of our blood with so much disrespect. He said Malcolm X knew the only real program for Black people lay in the area of Black unity, Black spiritual and intellectual awakening, Black leadership, and a Mau-Mau like commitment to change.

476. ________________. "Malcolm X and the Conscience of Black America," Liberator, Vol. 6, No. 2, February, 1966, pp. 10-11.

Author believes that the man they killed was no super hero, but a man with work to do. He concludes: "The

Spirit of which Malik El Shabazz is a part of must be infused in all activity that we consider meaningful and pertinent to the destiny of our people."

477. Newton, Huey P. "On Malcolm X," The Black Panther, March 7, 1970, p. 6.

The leader was quoted as saying: "The heirs of Malcolm X have picked up the gun and are moving for their total freedom."

478. Novack, George. "Malcolm X, Black Nationalism and Socialism," International Socialist Review, Vol. 28, No. 4, July-August, 1967, pp. 43-51.

Author gives an overview of Malcolm X's life and reviews George Breitman's The Last Year of Malcolm X: The Evolution of a Revolutionary.

479. "Now It's a Negro Drive for Segregation," U. S. News, Vol. 56, No. 13, March 30, 1964, pp. 38-39.

In this interview Malcolm X tells why integration will never work in the United States. He said it would not work because it doesn't solve the problem.

480. "Now It's Negroes vs. Negroes in America's Racial Violence," U. S. News, Vol. 58, No. 10, March 8, 1965, p. 6.

The writer discusses the assassination of Malcolm X. He said now it was Negroes killing other Negroes and not whites killing Negroes.

481. Nower, Joyce. "Cleaver's Vision of America and the New White Radical: A Legacy of Malcolm X," Negro American Literature Forum, Vol. 4, No. 1, March, 1970, pp. 12-21.

The author surmises that the new white radical has learned a lot about self-determination from the Black liberation struggle and from at least two of its most eloquent spokesmen---Malcolm X and, more recently (1970), Eldridge Cleaver.

482. O'Gara, James. "After Malcolm X," Commonweal, Vol. 82, No. 1, March 26, 1965, p. 8.

The writer discusses Malcolm X's impact on Black people and the Nation of Islam. He concludes: "But the headlines he received in life were a drop in the bucket compared to those he received in death-an ironic note which Malcolm would probably take as one more proof of the value of violence."

483. "Organize Rifle Club in Ohio: Malcolm X on the Scene," New York Amsterdam News, April 11, 1964, pp. 1, 2.

Malcolm X advised Negroes in Cleveland, Ohio to fight back as this city went through the worst racial disturbance in its history.

484. Parks, Gordon. "I Was a Zombie Then-Like All Muslims, I Was Hypnotized," Life, Vol. 58, No. 9, March 5, 1965, pp. 29-31.

The photographer-writer discusses the life and death of Malcolm X and his friendship with him.

485. ______________. "What Their Cry Means to Me-A Negro's Own Evaluation," Life, Vol. 54, No. 22, May 31, 1963, pp. 31-32, 78, 79.

The writer discusses his interview with Malcolm X. Malcolm X commented on a variety of topics: Black Muslims, NAACP, Elijah Muhammad, Martin Luther King, Jr., Supreme Court, "Bull" Connor, Robert Kennedy, etc.

486. "Peking and Malcolm X," New Republic, Vol. 152, No. 13, March 27, 1965, p. 8.

The writer states that Malcolm X was made a Chinese Communist martyr. He also suggests that Malcolm has his name inscribed in the Mythology of World Revolution.

487. Phillips, Waldo B. "Pied Piper of Harlem," Christian Century, Vol. 81, No. 14, April 1, 1964, pp. 422-423.

The author suggests that Negroes who pick up Malcolm X and use him temporarily as a club to intimidate Congress will discover that win or lose they will not easily put him down again.

488. Plimpton, George. "Miami Notebook: Cassius Clay and Malcolm X," Harper's Magazine, Vol. 228, No. 1369, June, 1964, pp. 54-61.

The writer interviewed Malcolm X during the Clay-Liston fight when he was in Miami. Malcolm X commented on a variety of issues: Martin Luther King, Jr., Supreme Court, Elijah Muhammad, Nonviolence, etc.

489. Porter, Herman. "Jurors Are Selected in Malcolm X Case," The Militant, January 24, 1966, p. 2.

490. ______________. "D. A. Presents Case in Malcolm X Trial," The Militant, January 31, 1966, pp. 1, 3.

491. ______________. "Malcolm X Murder Trial," The Militant, February 7, 1966, p. 2.

492. ______________. "Little Light Shed By Malcolm X Murder Trial," The Militant, February 14, 1966, pp. 1, 3.

493. ______________. "Police Give Testimony in Malcolm X Murder Trial," The Militant, February 21, 1966, p. 2.

494. ______________. "Defense Opens Case in Malcolm X Murder Trial," The Militant, February 28, 1966, p. 3.

495. Porter, Herman. "Confession Rocks Malcolm X Trial," The Militant, March 7, 1966, pp. 1, 4.

496. ______________. "Summary of Testimony in Malcolm X Murder Trial," The Militant, March 14, 1966, p. 3.

497. ______________. "Who Killed Malcolm X?," The Militant, March 21, 1966, pp. 1, 5.

498. "Previously Unpublished Remarks by Malcolm X," The Militant, May 24, 1965, p. 4.

This is a transcribed tape from remarks made by Malcolm X on January 7, 1965 at the Militant Labor Forum Meeting in New York.

499. "Program of Organization of Afro-American Unity," The Militant, July 13, 1964, p. 2.

This is the full text of the Statement of Basic Aims and Objectives of the Organization of Afro-American Unity made public by Malcolm X.

500. Protz, Roger. "Real Reason Why Malcolm X Went to Africa," Sepia, Vol. 13, No. 9, October, 1964, pp. 42-46.

The author surmises that Malcolm X's trip is the first real attempt to gain acceptance for America's Black Muslims from the orthodox Islamic world. He concludes: "If Malcolm succeeds, he may well convert (Elijah) Muhammad's dissident followers into a powerful force for racial equality rather than racial hate."

501. "Postscript on the Assassination of Malcolm X," Black Collegian, Vol. 35, No. 4, December, 1980, p. 66.

The writer points out that Malcolm X's assassination was a loss to the Civil Rights Movement.

502. "Reactionaries on the Verge of Extinction Invariably Conduct a Last Desperate Struggle," The Black Panther, March 15, 1970, p. 8.

Article states that the spirit of Malcolm X lives in the will of the people to be free and no reactionaries can kill his ideas.

503. "Remember the Words of Brother Malcolm," The Black Panther, May 18, 1968, pp. 1, 6, 7.

The author declares: "Malcolm lives through his spirit. His legacy is the direction he gave to revolution, to the people. In demanding a United Nations-supervised plebescite, in which only Black colonialized subjects participate, our spirit and drive and the spirit and legacy of Malcolm X forge into one powerful revolutionary thrust."

504. "Renounces Racism, Calls Black Muslim Leader Elijah Muhammad a Religious 'Faker' and Says He Will Work To 'Undo Harm I Did To So Many Well-Meaning, Innocent Negroes Who Believe in Muhammad Because of 'My Own Evangelistic Zeal'; Holds He Is Now Orthodox Moslem," New York Times, October 4, 1964, p. 59.

Malcolm X denounces the leader of the Nation of Islam and called him a fake.

505. Richmond, Norman "Otis". "Malcolm X: Toronto Connection," Contrast (Toronto, Canada), May 1, 1981, p. 18.

Author states very little has been written about Malcolm X's visit to Toronto, Canada, on January 19, 1965, only weeks before his assassination on February 21, 1965. Toronto is where he had his last television appearance before his death.

506. Ring, Harry. "Interview with James Shabazz," The Militant, March 8, 1965, p. 3.

Mr. James Shabazz was Malcolm X's personal secretary. He commented on a number of issues including Malcolm X's death, his family, Black leadership and the future of the Organization for Afro-American Unity.

507. __________. "Malcolm X Maps Campaign to Build Black Nationalism," The Militant, March 16, 1962, p. 1.

In an interview with Mr. Ring, Malcolm told him of his social, political and economic plans to help uplift Blacks. Malcolm asserts, in part: "I am prepared to cooperate in local civil-rights actions in the South and elsewhere...every campaign for specific objectives can only heighten the political consciousness of the Negroes and intensify their identification against white societies."

508. __________. "Malcolm X Starts Movement in Harlem for All Negroes," The Militant, March 23, 1964, pp. 1, 6.

Malcolm X established a Muslim Mosque in Harlem that would also permit Negroes who were not Muslims to participate in the political, economic and social programs. He said that while his group was pro-Black this did not mean it was anti-white.

509. __________. "Radio Interview with Malcolm X," The Militant, February 8, 1965, p. 3.

This is the text of a discussion with Malcolm X over radio station WBAI-FM in New York on January 28, 1965.

510. Robertson, Bill. "Elijah Muhammad: America's No. 1 Black Supremacist," Bronze America, Vol. 1, December, 1964, pp. 20-25.

Author mentions Malcolm X's role in the Nation of Islam.

511. Robinson, Cedric J. "Malcolm Little as a Charismatic Leader," Afro-American Studies, Vol. 3, No. 1, September, 1972, pp. 81-96.

The writer gives an overview of Malcolm X's life. Professor Robinson also points out: "...The bitterness of Malcolm X was understated for he clearly looked upon the Nation (of Islam) as his own creation despite his oft-repeated denials...."

512. Robinson, Jackie. "Bullets Silenced a Man of Courage," Michigan Chronicle, March 13, 1965.

Writer comments on Malcolm X's assassination. He suggests that the leader was a man of convictions.

513. Robinson, Louie. "Redd Foxx-Crown Prince of Clowns," Ebony, Vol. 22, No. 6, April, 1967, pp. 91-92, 94, 96, 98.

In this article Redd Foxx recalls his friendship with Malcolm X. Foxx met him in the 1940's in Chicago. Maclom's nickname in those years was "Detroit Red," states Foxx.

514. Robinson, Patricia. "Malcolm X, Our Revolutionary Son and Brother," Malcolm X: The Man and His Times, John Henrik Clarke, Editor, pp. 56-63.

The author concludes, in part: "...with the widsom born from the betrayal of the Black father and his own individual revolution against tyranny, Malcolm turned to the poor masses, the women and the young people...."

515. "Rockwell Gets Warning from Malcolm X," The Militant, February 1, 1965, p. 8.

Malcolm X sent a telegram to George Lincoln Rockwell, head of the American Nazi Party. He told him that if harm came to Martin Luther King, Jr. in Alabama by him or his group, that his group would be met with maximum physical retaliation....

516. Rossa, Della. "L. A. Muslims Get White 'Justice'," The Militant, June 24, 1963, p. 8.

Malcolm X declares that convicted Muslims were victims of brutality and that it was cops who should have been on trial.

517. Russell, Carlos E. "Exclusive Interview with Brother Malcolm X," Liberator, Vol. 4, No. 5, May, 1964, pp. 12-13.

In this interview Malcolm X argues that what he means by Black Nationalism is that the Black man must control the politics of his own community. He concludes: "I also mean that we (Black people) must do those things necessary to elevate ourselves socially, culturally, and to restore racial dignity."

518. Rustin, Bayard. "On Malcolm X," New America, February 28, 1965, pp. 1, 8.

The writer suggests that Malcolm was a help to established civil rights organizations, because he frightened white people into negotiating with Dr. King and James Farmer...He also surmises: "White America, not the Negro people, will determine Malcolm X's role in history."

519. Samuel, Gertrude. "Feud Within the Black Muslims," New York Times, May 22, 1964, pp. 26-29.

The feud discussed was between Malcolm X and Elijah Muhammad.

520. Saunders, Lois. "L. A. Negro Community Unites in Defense of Black Muslims," The Militant, May 21, 1962, p. 2.

Malcolm X was in Los Angeles and spoke to Negroes at the Second Baptist Church. He urged solidarity of Negro, Mexican-American and other minority groups to combat police terror.

521. Sax, Janet Cheatham. "Malik El Shabazz: A Survey of His Interpreters," Black Scholar, Vol. 1, No. 7, May, 1970, pp. 51-55.

The writer gives an overview of Malcolm X's philosophy. She concludes: "Malcolm, of course, comprehended the economical class analysis of capitalist society, knew racial oppression in all its aspects, and certainly did not feel the necessity of any black/white alliance before he could be about the business of Black liberation."

522. Schroth, Raymond. "Malcolm X Is Alive," America, Vol. 116, No. 16, April 22, 1967, p. 594.

The writer suggests that Malcolm X is alive through his autobiography. He believes that his autobiography can be read as a religious testimony; at the same time, it is a mercilessly exorcizing indictment of American private morality.

523. ________________. "The Redemption of Malcolm X," Catholic World, Vol. 205, No. 1,230, September, 1967, pp. 346-352.

Malcolm X, according to Father Schroth, experienced grace and evil so intensely and so publicly that "as a human and efficacious sign to all men, his life took on cosmic significance." The writer also suggests "his greatest virtue was his openness to reality."

524. Seraile, William. "Malcolm X and David Walker: Brothers in Radical Thought," Black World, Vol. 22, No. 12, October, 1973, pp. 68-73.

The author argues that both Malcolm X and David Walker were men of vision and understood that complete liberation would never come as long as some worked with the power structure to keep the masses down, while others were so eager to "make it" for themselves that they quickly forgot where they came from.

525. ________________. "The Assassination of Malcolm X: The View from Home and Abroad," Afro-Americans in New York Life and History, Vo. 5, No. 1, January, 1981, pp. 43-58.

526. Shabazz, Betty. "Malcolm X as a Husband and Father," Malcolm X: The Man and His Times, John Henrik Clarke, Editor, pp. 132-143.

His wife concludes: "Malcolm was the greatest thing in my life and he taught me what every female ought to learn: to live and to love as a woman, to be true to myself and my responsibilities as a mother. And to use my spiritual, material, and intellectual capacities to help build a better human society...."

527. ______________. "The Legacy of My Husband, Malcolm X," Ebony, Vol. 24, No. 8, June, 1969, pp. 172-182.

His wife declares that Malcolm was killed because he would not compromise his principles, because he had become a threat to powerful interests in this country that favored to maintain the status quo.

528. Shapiro, Herbert. "The Education of Malcolm X," Jewish Currents, Vol. 20. October, 1966, pp. 6-11.

The author discusses how Malcolm X's philosophy changed over the years.

529. Smith, Baxter. "FBI Memos Reveal Repression Schemes," Black Scholar, Vol. 5, No. 7, April, 1974, pp. 43-48.

The writer implies that new facts now coming to light link the government to the murders of Malcolm X, Martin Luther King, Jr. and Fred Hampton. There is also a short section on Malcolm X.

530. Smith, Ed. and David Herman. "Meetings in Harlem Hear Malcolm X and Fannie Lou Hamer," The Militant, December 28, 1964, pp. 1, 2.

Malcolm X told the rally that it was necessary to study and understand the freedom struggle all over the world in order to win freedom here.

531. Snelling, Roland. "Malcolm X: As International Statesman," Liberator, Vol. 6, No. 2, February, 1966, pp. 6-9.

The writer shows how Malcolm X's trip abroad made him an international statesman. He traveled in Africa and the Middle East and met with the heads of states.

532. Southwick, Albert B. "Malcolm X: Charismatic Demagogue," Christian Century, Vol. 80, No. 23, June 5, 1963, pp. 740-741.

This is an interview with Malcolm X. He discusses a variety of topics: White Liberals, Martin Luther King, Jr., Black Muslims, NAACP. Mr. Southwick concludes: "If the dangerous sparks of Black racism being thrown off continually by Malcolm X should ever start a real conflagration among one-tenth of our citizens, our past racial troubles will seem like child's play."

533. Spellman, A. B. "An Interview with Malcolm X," Rhythm Magazine, Vol. 1, No. 2, 1970, pp. 2-7.

In 1964, Mr. Spellman questions Malcolm X on his reasons for leaving the Nation of Islam, his current political/economic philosophies, and his plans for Black Nationalism within the United States. The interviewer concludes: "If he (Malcolm X) had lived, he would have built the OAAU (Organization of Afro-American Unity) into the greatest Pan-African political party ever seen on this continent. He could have pulled us all. And that has to be why he was killed."

534. ______________. "Black Nationalism and Radical Unity," Second Coming, Vol. 1, January, 1965, pp. 10-12.

Malcolm X as a leader in Harlem, New York, is discussed.

535. ______________. "Interview with Malcolm X," Monthly Review, Vol. 16, No. 1, May, 1964, pp. 14-24.

Malcolm X commented on a number of topics. He said there is hostility between Black and white working classes because the working class whites have been just as much against not only working class Blacks, but all Blacks, period.

536. ______________. "The Legacy of Malcolm X," Liberator, Vol. 5, No. 6, June, 1965, pp. 11-13.

The writer concludes that Malcolm X's death should teach Black people two things, (1) from here on it must be organization and not personality and (2) there are elements in the Black community which can be used to do the fascist's work.

537. ______________. "Malcolm X on the Black Revolution in U.S.A.," Revolution, Vol. 1, No. 12, April, 1964, pp. 23-31.

The same article was published simultaneously in the May, 1964 issue of Monthly Review. See above citation.

538. Spitz, Barry N. "The End of Malcolm X," Sepia, Vol. 14, No. 5, May, 1965, pp. 14-17.

It was pointed out that it was an ironic twist and perhaps prophetic that the last words on the lips of Malcolm X was "brothers". He spoke the word for the last time while calling for peace between two Negroes who may have been part of a plot that took his life as he stood on the stage of the Audubon Ballroom in Harlem, states the article.

539. Stafford, M. L. "Jail Term for Black Muslim Arrested While Selling Paper," The Militant, February 4, 1963, p. 8.

Malcolm X conferred with New York City officials on the problems of police brutality against Negroes.

540. Sykes, Ossie. "The Week That Malcolm X Died," Liberator, Vol. 5, No. 4, April, 1965, pp. 4-7.

The writer discusses the events that took place in New York and elsewhere the week when Malcolm X was killed. He states that some 30,000 people visited the Unity Funeral Home to pay homage to Malcolm.

541. "Telephone Conversation (Between Malcolm X and Carlos Moore)," Malcolm X: The Man and His Times, John Henrik Clarke, Editor, pp. 205-211.

This conversation between Malcolm and the Afro-Cuban nationalist Carlos Moore occurred on February 9, 1965. Malcolm X was in London after having been barred from entering Paris. Carlos Moore was in Paris.

542. "Ten Greats of Black History," Ebony, Vol. 27, August, 1972, p. 40.

Malcolm X is included in this list. The article stated that partron saint of the Black consciousness movement of the 1960's and 1970's, Malcolm X represented the tremendous integrity of the new Black man, willing to know himself, to love himself, to be profoundly critical of himself and, at the same time, to know the enemy and to speak truthfully about the Black situation in America.

543. "Text of Speech by James Shabazz," The Militant, March 15, 1965, p. 3.

This is the text of speech that Mr. Shabazz delivered on March 5, 1965 at the Militant Labor Forum Memorial Meeting for Malcolm X.

544. "Text of Statement by Malcolm X," The Militant, March 23, 1964, p. 6.

This is the text of the statement made by Malcolm X in opening his press conference at New York's Park-Sheraton Hotel, March 12, 1964. He declared, in part: "Our political philosophy will be Black Nationalism. Our economic and social philosophy will be Black Nationalism. Our cultural emphasis will be Black Nationalism...."

545. "The Changing Ideas of Malcolm X," Transition (Howard University), Vol. 1, No. 2, 1972, pp. 80-92.

Article discusses how Malcolm X's philosophy changed over the years.

546. "The Life of Malcolm X," Sacramento Observer, May 18, 1972, p. A-6.

This article gives a brief overview of Malcolm X's three distinct and interrelated lives, as Malcolm Little, Malcolm X, and Eli-Hajj Malik El-Shabazz.

547. Thomas, Norman. "Tragedy of Malcolm X," America, Vol. 112, No. 2, March 6, 1965, pp. 303-304.

The writer concludes: "From the Malcolm X tragedy, Negroes will learn the futility of mere hate. Whites must learn to change-both thoroughly and swiftly-the type of world that makes frustration and bitterness the daily bread of so many millions...."

548. Thomas, Tony. "Malcolm X and the Civil Rights Struggle," The Militant, Vol. 35, No. 22, June 11, 1971, p. 8.

The writer compares Malcolm X's strategy in the Civil Rights struggle with that of other Black leaders, particularly Martin Luther King, Jr.

549. ____________. "The Strategy of Malcolm X for Black Liberation," The Militant, Vol. 28, No. 20, May, 1971, p. 9.

The writer surmises: "The strategy of Malcolm X has been supported and expanded by the Socialist Workers Party in its 'Transitional Program for Black Liberation' adopted in 1969, and embodies the course that the new generation of Black rebels is following...."

550. "2,000 Hear Malcolm X in Cleveland," The Militant, April 13, 1964, pp. 1, 3.

Malcolm devoted a major part of his speech exposing and castigating the Democratic Party.

551. "United States: Armed Confrontation," The Black Panther, November 15, 1969, p. 13.

States that the forerunner of Afro-American struggle was Malcolm X, who correctly viewed the road of armed struggle as the only one leading to the destruction of the U. S. racist and imperialist power structure.

552. "U. S. Black Nationalist Leader Malcolm X to Attend (Organization of African Unity) Meeting Observer," New York Times, July 14, 1964, p. 23.

553. Vernon, Robert. "A 'Left-Wing' Smear of Malcolm X," The Militant, May 24, 1965, p. 3; May 30, 1965, p. 3.

The writer comments on an article by Bayard Rustin and Tom Kahn on Malcolm X that appeared in the March 24 issue of New America.

554. ______________. "James Wechsler's Attack on Malcolm X: Why Black Nationalism Upsets Liberals," The Militant, June 22, 1964, p. 5.

555. ______________. "Malcolm X, Voice of the Black Ghetto," International Socialist Review, Vol. 26, No. 2, Spring, 1965, pp. 36-37.

The author concludes: "Malcolm X lived as a revolutionist, died as a revolutionist, and at his death was developing into a more effective revolutionist, on a local and on an internationalist scale, in the fight for Black people in America and in the fight for the oppressed all over the world."

556. ______________. "Violent End of the Man Called Malcolm X," Life, Vol. 58, No. 9, March 5, 1965, pp. 26-27.

This article includes closeup photoes of Malcolm X as he lay wounded.

557. Walker, Wyatt Tee. "Nothing But a Man," Negro Digest, Vol. 14, No. 10, August, 1965, pp. 29-32.

The author discusses Malcolm X along with a number of Black leaders: Martin Luther King, Jr., Jesse Gray, Milton Galamison, and Elijah Muhammad. He surmises: "He was the symbol of Negro males who, though groping, have not yet found the answer to how they can be 'nothing but a man', which is, really, more than enough."

558. Warde, William. "The Life and Death of Malcolm X," International Socialist Review, Vol. 26, No. 2, Spring, 1965, pp. 35-36.

The writer observes: "His sensitivity enabled him to establish instant communion with oppressed millions who impatiently await the emancipation and equality they have been promised....Malcolm X, whose memory they can patronize now that he has been silenced, was the herald and authentic spokesman...."

559. Warren, Robert Penn. "Malcolm X: Mission and Meaning," Yale Review, Vol. 56, No. 2, Winter, 1967, pp. 161-171.

The writer suggests that The Autobiography of Malcolm X has permanence and that it has something of tragic intensity and meaning. One feels that it is an American story bound to be remembered....

560. Watts, Daniel. "Malcolm X: The Unfulfilled Promise," Liberator, Vol. 5, No. 3, March, 1965, p. 3.

This editorial is an obituary to Malcolm X by the writer. He concludes: "The crime and tragedy of the present 'responsible' civil rights leaders will be, if they fail to get the message in Malcolm's death, that the present direction in which they are leading our struggle, is doomed to the garbage heap and the graveyard that is America."

561. ____________. "Malcolm X vs. White Press," Liberator, Vol. 6, No. 3, March, 1966, p. 3.

This editorial asserts we cannot expect factual or honest reporting from the white press on activities in the Black ghettoes. He states that it can be seen by the white press putting Malcolm down.

562. ____________. "The Last 'Spokesman'," Liberator, Vol. 6, No. 2, February, 1966, p. 3.

This editorial concludes that Malcolm, for his brief movement on the stage of history as spokesman for the wretched of the earth, articulated more soulfully and forcefully the sufferings and the lower depths, to which Black Americans have been consigned, than any other Black man in the last 40 years.

563. Wechsler, James A. "Malcolm X and the Death of Rev. Klunder," New York Post, April 13, 1964.

564. ________________. "The Cult of Malcolm X," Progressive, Vol. 28, No. 6, June, 1964, pp. 24-28.

The writer declares, in part: "...Malcolm X and his disciples are equally removed from reality when they advertise salvation in autonomous ghettoes, and incite total war against the white community...."

565. ________________. "Who Issued the Orders?," Newsweek, Vol. 67, No. 12, March 21, 1966, p. 36.

The writer discusses Malcolm X's assassination. He asked the question, who killed Malcolm X? The writer also discusses the role of the three defendants in the assassination and concludes: "The Malcolm X murder case was closed-without the name of the general who gave the orders to the firing squad."

566. ________________. "Why Black Muslims Are Focusing on the Nation's Capital Now," U. S. News, Vol. 54, No. 54, May 27, 1963, p. 24.

The article states that Malcolm X spread the message of the Black Muslims in Washington, D. C. Malcolm X states that his chief purpose was to attack juvenile delinquency in the Capital.

567. ________________. "Why Malcolm X Quit the Black Muslims," Sepia, Vol. 13, No. 5, May, 1964, pp. 58-61.

The writer asserts that when Malcolm broke with the Black Muslims, he hinted that Elijah Muhammad's sons and daughters had resented the power and popularity he had gained during the ten years he had served as Muhammad's second in command. The writer concludes: "Only time and history will record if he exerted an influence for good or ill upon the progress of the American Negro."

568. "Where Is the American Negro Headed?," Malcolm X: The Man and His Times, John Henrik Clarke, Editor, pp. 149-167.

This is a transcript of the "Open Mind" program broadcast over NBC television, October 15, 1961. The guests included: Monroe Berger, Kenneth B. Clark, Richard Haley, Constance B. Motley and Malcolm X. At this time Malcolm was the public spokesman for the Black Muslims.

569. White, Butch. "Remembrance: Malcolm X," Black World, Vol. 24, No. 7, May, 1975, pp. 88-89.

The writer hopes that we should not forget Malcolm X or lose sight of his visions.

570. White, Milton CMSgt. "Malcolm X in the Military," Black Scholar, Vol. 1, No. 7, May, 1970, pp. 31-35.

The author states that to the American Armed Forces, Malcolm X was born March 10, 1970. That was the day two Air Force chief master sergeants took a document bearing his name into the office of a white commanding officer, setting off a reaction that reached from that room to the White House. He discusses how they wanted to organize the Malcolm X Association at Vandenberg Air Force Base.

571. Whitehurst, James Emerson. "The Mainstreaming of the Black Muslims: Healing the Hate," Christian Century, Vol. 47, February 27, 1980, pp. 225-229.

States that under Malcolm X's leadership the number of Muslim centers increased from 40 to well over 100.

572. Wiley, Charles W. "Who Was Malcolm X?," National Review, Vol. 17, March 23, 1965, pp. 239-240.

The writer, a white man, feels the stereotyped image given by the press to Malcolm X does him less than justice. He also discusses several interviews that he had with Malcolm X.

573. Wilson, Charles E. "Leadership: Triumph in Leadership Tragedy," Malcolm X: The Man and His Times, John Henrik Clarke, Editor, pp. 27-41.

The writer observes that Malcolm X's death and failures were tragic. Wilson concludes: "But as one of current history's great figures, Malcolm's mistakes, shortcomings and all, triumphed over his personal tragedy...."

574. ________________ and Ossie Sykes. "Malcolm X: A Tragedy of Leadership," Liberator, May 1965, pp. 7-11.

The writers surmise that Malcolm X's death marked the end of prospects that the Negro revolution might become revolutionary....The new leaders may have an opportunity to learn from Malcolm X's experience, conclude the authors.

575. ________________. "The Quotable Mr. X," Liberator, May, 1965, pp. 11-13.

The writer gives statements by Malcolm X on such issues as: "On white America," "On Black America," "On The Overseas Arena."

576. Winfrey, Charles. "The Evolution of Malcolm X: From Poseur to Pan-Africanist," Mazungumzo, Vol. 2, No. 3, 1972, pp. 74-82.

The author gives an overview of Malcolm X's life. He concludes: "Malcolm X left an undying legacy. His words, his values, his determination, his spirit, his ideas, and his love will be the bricks and mortar for the new Black nation to come."

577. Worthy, William. "Malcolm X Says Group Will Stress Politics," National Guardian, March 21, 1964.

Malcolm X points out that his organization would get involved in politics.

5.
General Articles About Malcolm X

A Selected List

578. Adams, Alvin. "Malcolm X 'Seemed Sincere' About Helping Cause: Mrs. King," Jet, March 11, 1965.

579. Baldwin, James. "Letter from a Region in My Mind," New Yorker, Vol. 38, No. 39, November 17, 1962, pp. 100, 102, 127.

580. Barbee, Bobbie E. "Will Link with Malcolm X Harm Clay's Career-Champ Offers $20,000 to Anyone Changing His Muslim's Beliefs," Jet, March 26, 1964, p. 50.

581. Bartlett, Charles. "Malcolm X, An Angry Extremist," Washington Evening Star, July 28, 1964.

582. "Bayard Rustin Sees 'Malcolm X-ism' Inevitable Unless Nation Ends Racial Injustice," New York Times, March 4, 1965, p. 32.

583. "BBC Scored for Allegedly Conducting Malcolm X, U.S. Negro Nationalist, on Smethwick Tour," New York Times, February 14, 1965, p. 24.

584. "Benefit for Malcolm X Widow Friday Nite," New York Amsterdam News, April 24, 1965, p. 26.

585. Berger, Morroe. "The Black Muslims," Horizon, Winter, 1964, pp. 48-65.

586. Bigart, Homer. "Police on Alert over Muslim Rift," New York Times, June 18, 1964, p. 2.

587. "Black Muslim Denied Any Connection with Murder of Malcolm X," Wall Street Journal, February 23, 1965, pp. 1, 3.

588. "Black Muslim Leader Malcolm X Breaking with Movement's Leader Elijah Muhammad, Says He Is Forming Politically Oriented Black Nationalist Party," New York Times, March 9, 1964, p. 1.

589. "Black Muslim Leader Malcolm X, W. Ussery of CORE and D. Warden Urge Negroes to Improve Conditions by Their Own Efforts, Oakland Meeting Organized by Afro-American Association to Discuss Negroes' Future," New York Times, November 26, 1962, p. 18.

590. "Black Muslims Assault the People at Malcolm X Festival Held at Philadelphia Community College," The Black Panther, March 7, 1970, pp. 7, 16.

591. "Black Muslim Leader Malcolm X Reports Negro Registration Planned at NYC Rally," New York Times, March 23, 1964, p. 18.

592. "Black Muslims Press Drive to Separate Races; Malcolm X, Chicago," New York Times, February 28, 1963, p. 5.

593. "Black Muslims' Temple No. 7 in Harlem Renamed for Malcolm X for His Great Work When He Was with Nation of Islam-Move Reflects Acceptance of Slain Ex-Leader," New York Times, February 2, 1976, pp. 1, 14.

594. Blackman, M. C. "8 Guards, 32 Police for Malcolm X," New York Tribune, June 16, 1964.

595. "Blood Bath on Way Here, Malcolm X Tells English," Afro-American, July 18, 1964, p. 1.

596. Boggs, James. "Malcolm X Inquiry Stirs Harlem," Now!, Vol. 2, January, 1966, p. 14.

597. Booker, James. "Malcolm X Ignores Brother," New York Amsterdam News, April 4, 1964, pp. 1, 2.

598. Borden, Karen Wells. "The Black Rhetoric in the 1960's: Sociohistorical Perspectives," Journal of Black Studies, Vol. 3, No. 4, 1973, pp. 423-431.

599. Bradley, Edward. "Driver Tells How Malcolm X Escaped Death in Chase," Washington Evening Star, February 24, 1965, pp. A-1, 6.

600. ______________ as told to Louis E. Lomax. "Malcolm Escaped Killers in Los Angeles by James Bond-Type Ruse," Patterson Morning Call, February 25, 1965.

601. Breslin, Jimmy. "Police Rescue Two Suspects in Murder of Malcolm X," New York Herald Tribune, February 22, 1965, p. 1.

602. "Brother's Plea Started Malcolm X in Muslims," Washington Evening Star, February 22, 1965, p. A-3.

603. "Buckley, Lane and Malcolm X at CCNY Student Meeting," New York Times, December 8, 1961, p. 28.

604. Buckley, Thomas. "Defense Is Opened in Malcolm Case: Promises to Prove Accused Were Not at Killing," New York Times, February 22, 1966, p. 1.

605. ______________. "Malcolm Witness Claims Innocence," New York Times, March 2, 1966, p. 50.

606. Byrd, Earl. "Malcolm X's Wife: The Bicentennial Is for Blacks, Too," Washington Star, June 29, 1976, pp. B-1, 4.

607. Carmack, George. "Two Roads for Selma Negroes: Love or Violence," New York World-Telegram and Sun, February 5, 1965, p. 2.

608. Carroll, Maurice C. "The Near-Battle of Black Muslims," New York Tribune, June 18, 1964.

609. Casey, Phil. "Crowd Appears, Elijah Doesn't at Muslim Rally," Washington Post, June 26, 1961, p. A-3.

610. "Cassius X," Newsweek, Vol. 63, March 16, 1964, p. 74.

Article mentions that Malcolm X accompanied Cassius X on his tour of Harlem, New York.

611. "Cathy White and Malcolm X," New York Amsterdam News, February 27, 1965, p. 47.

612. Charles, Irah M. "Malcolm X's Widow (Betty Shabazz) Calls for Racial Reassessment," Michigan Chronicle, June 6, 1970, p. 4.

613. Cleage, Albert B. Jr. "The Next Step: An Analysis of the Black Revolution," The Illustrated News (Detroit), May 4, 1964.

614. "Church Says It Did Not Refuse Malcolm," New York Amsterdam News, March 6, 1965, p. 2.

615. Collins, Mrs. Ella. "Why Malcolm X Had to Die Among His People - A Sister's View," Afro-American, February 24, 1968, pp. 1-2.

616. "Concerned Mothers Mutual Benefit Committee Enlists Aid of Negro and White Artists in Raising $5,000 Toward $40,000 Goal for House of Mrs. Betty Shabazz, Wife of Late Malcolm X," New York Times, August 9, 1965, p. E-8.

617. "Council of African Organizations (CAO) in London Stages a Protest Demonstration Against U. S. Racialist Murder of Malcolm X," West Africa, March 6, 1965, p. 273.

618. "D. C. Lawyer (Edward Bennett Williams) to Handle Appeal of 3 Convicted in Malcolm X Murder," The Militant, September 26, 1966, p. 4.

619. DeBerry, Clifton. "DeBerry Denounces Threat to Malcolm X by N. Y. Cops," The Militant, March 23, 1964, p. 6.

620. "Defense on in (Malcolm) X Trial," New York Amsterdam News, February 26, 1966, p. 1.

621. "Dick Gregory Hails Malcolm X's Stand," The Militant, April 20, 1964, p. 8.

622. "Domestic Peace Corps Speaker-Malcolm X," New York Tribune, December 10, 1964.

623. Dudar, Helen. "The Muslims and Black Nationalism," Part 1, New York Post, April 6, 1964, p. 21.

624. ___________. "The Muslims and Black Nationalism," Part 2, New York Post, April 7, 1964, p. 29.

625. ___________. "The Muslims and Black Nationalism," Part 3, New York Post, April 8, 1964, p. 41.

626. ___________. "The Muslims and Black Nationalism," Part 4, New York Post, April 9, 1964, p. 27.

627. ___________. "The Muslims and Black Nationalism: What Does Malcolm Want?," Part 5, New York Post, April 12, 1964, p. 25.

628. ___________. "The Muslims and Black Nationalism," Part 6, New York Post, April 12, 1964, p. 25.

629. ___________. "The Return of Malcolm X," New York Times, May 22, 1964, p. 91.

630. Dunayenskaya, Roya. "Malcolm X and 'Old Radical'," News and Letters (Detroit), April, 1964.

631. Duodu, Cameron. "Malcolm X: Prophet of Harlem," Drum Magazine, Ghana edition, October, 1964.

632. Editorial. "Bayard Rustin and Malcolm X," The Militant, March 15, 1965, p. 4.

633. Editorial. "Elijah Muhammad's (Malcolm X) Mao," New York Tribune, March 10, 1964.

634. Editorial. "To Arms with Malcolm X," New York Times, March 14, 1964.

635. Editorial. "What Killed Malcolm X," Weekly People, March 13, 1965.

636. Edmonson, Locksley. "The Internationalization of Black Power: Historical and Comtemporary Perspectives," Mawazo, Vol. 1, December, 1968, pp. 16-30.

Author sees the evolution of the Black Power Movement through leaders as Malcolm X, Marcus Garvey, W. E. B. DuBois, Martin Luther King, Jr., and others.

637. El-Amin, Hassan. "Malcolm X's Alleged Killer Speaks Out," New York Amsterdam News, January 14, 1978, pp. 1, 7.

638. "Elijah Muhammad Suspends Malcolm X," New York Amsterdam News, December 7, 1963, p. 1.

639. Ellenberg, Albert. "Elijah Muhammad Weeps for Loss of Malcolm X," New York Post, March 10, 1964.

640. ________. "Malcolm Bolts the Muslims-Without (Cassius) Clay," New York Post, March 9, 1964.

641. "Enter Muhammad?," National Review, Vol. 14, July 2, 1963, p. 520.

642. "Exonerate Malcolm X: Kenyatta," New York Amsterdam News, June 3, 1975, p. A-14.

643. "Fire Sweeps Mosque of Harlem Muslims: Malcolm X Slaying Link Indicated," Washington Evening Star, February 23, 1965, p. 1.

644. "George Barner and Malcolm X," New York Amsterdam News, February 27, 1965, p. 3.

645. Hall, Gordon D. "Malcolm X: The Man and the Myth," Boston Sunday Herald, February 28, 1965.

646. Halstead, Fred. "He Would Not Bow His Head to Any Tyrant," The Militant, March 8, 1965, pp. 1, 5.

647. Handler, M. S. "Farmer Says Mood of Negroes Is One of Growing Militancy," New York Times, February 10, 1966, p. 41.

648. ________. "Malcolm X Cites Progress of Jews: Says It Can Provide Lesson for American Negroes," New York Times, May 24, 1964, p. 91.

649. ________. "Malcolm X Pleased by Whites' Attitude on Trip to Mecca," New York Times, May 8, 1964, pp. 1, 38.

650. ________. "Malcolm X Seeks U. N. Negro Debate: He Asks African States to Cite U. S. Over Rights," New York Times, August 13, 1964, p. 135.

651. "Harlem Is Bracing for Muslim Rally," New York Amsterdam News, June 29, 1963, pp. 1. 2.

652. "Harlem, NYC, Hospital and Social Worker Seek Advice from Black Muslim Leader Malcolm X on Secret Therapy to Rehabilitate Alcoholics after Claims of Phenomenal Successes," New York Times, January 10, 1964, p. 84.

653. Haywood, J. W. Jr. "Honoring King, Malcolm X," Washington Post, February 2, 1974.

Letter to the Editor declaring that there should be no national holiday for Malcolm X.

654. Henriksen, Thomas H. "Edward W. Blyden: His Influence on Comtemporary Afro-Americans," Pan-African Journal, Summer, 1971, pp. 255-265.

Author discusses Blyden's influence on Malcolm X and others' ideas.

655. "Hit Malcolm X as 'Judas', Brother Accuses His Brother of Betraying Aides," Chicago Defender, March 28, 1964, p. 1.

656. "How Blacks Remember Malcolm X," Jet, May 20, 1970, pp. 22-28.

657. "How the World Saw Malcolm X's Death," New York Amsterdam News, March 13, 1965, p. 6.

658. Hunt, Frank. "Malcolm X Still Lives," Baltimore Afro-American, February 19, 1966.

659. Hunter, Clarence. "Dissident Muslim Expected to Be 'Silenced Forever'," Washington Evening Star, February 22, 1965, pp. A-1, 4.

660. "'I Killed Malcolm'-Hagan," New York Amsterdam News, March 5, 1966, p. 1.

661. "I'll Tell It All--Malcolm X's Widow," New York Amsterdam News, February 19, 1966, p. 1.

662. "Indicted in Slaying (of Malcolm X)," New York Amsterdam News, March 13, 1965, p. 2.

663. "The Inside Story of the Malcolm X Is 201 Memorial," New York Amsterdam News, march 2, 1968.

664. "James Baldwin, Martin Luther King, Jr., and Malcolm X Accused President Kennedy of Inadequate Leadership, in Two Interviews," New York Times, June 25, 1963, p. 13.

665. "James Baldwin, Martin Luther King, Jr., and Malcolm X Differ on Negro Tactics, in TV Interview; Malcolm X Scores King on Integration; Baldwin Holds Black Muslims Teach Negroes False Sense of Superiority," New York Times, June 25, 1963, p. 13.

666. Jones, Theodore. "Malcolm X Knew He Was a 'Marked Man'," New York Times, February 22, 1966, p. 16.

667. Kempton, Murray. "Malcolm X," Spectator (London), February 26, 1965.

668. "King Views Malcolm X as Tragic," New York Amsterdam News, March 28, 1964.

669. Kirk, Russell. "Malcolm X's Promise Was Murdered Too," Detroit Free Press, March 2, 1965.

670. Kirsch, Robert R. "The Real and Imagined Faces of Malcolm X," Los Angeles Times, November 5, 1965.

671. "Lawyers Say Malcolm Was Poisoned," New York Amsterdam News, March 13, 1965, p. 4.

672. Lelyveld, Joseph. "Elijah Muhammad Rallies His Followers in Harlem," New York Times, June 29, 1964, pp. 1, 32.

673. Lerner, Max. "Malcolm X and 'White Devils'," Detroit News, March 16, 1964.

674. __________. "White Devils?," New York Post, March 9, 1964, p. 39.

675. "Les Mathews and Malcolm X," New York Amsterdam News, February 27, 1965, p. 47.

676. Lester, Julius. "The Angry Children of Malcolm X," Sing Out!, Vol. 16, October-November, 1966, pp. 20-25.

677. "Letters to Editor About Malcolm X's Death," The Militant, March 15, 1965, p. 7.

678. Lewis, Jesse W. Jr. "Man Who 'Tamed' Malcolm Is Hopeful," Los Angeles Times, May 17, 1964.

679. Lomax, Almena. "Notes on a Nationalist's Death," The Tribune (Los Angeles), March 15, 1965.

680. "Louis E. Lomax to Write a 'Dramatic Treatment' of Life of Malcolm X for a 20th Century-Fox Movie," Jet, December 7, 1967, p. 45.

681. Lubell, Samuel. "Did Malcolm's Ironic Role Advance Rights?," Detroit Free Press, March 1, 1965.

682. Major, Clarence. "Malcolm X," Nation, Vol. 200, No. 10, March 8, 1965, p. 239.

683. "Malcolm Ordered to Move From Black Muslim House," New York Times, September 3, 1964, p. 16.

684. "Malcolm: Revered for Honesty," Sacramento Observer, May 21, 1970, p. 11.

685. "Malcolm Says He Is Backed Abroad," New York Times, May 22, 1964, p. 22.

686. "Malcolm Says Muhammad Fails Cause of Negro," New York Times, June 20, 1964, p. 101.

687. "Malcolm Sees Evil Choice at Polls," New York Post, September 8, 1964, p. 12.

688. "Malcolm Told Cops of Plot to Kill Him," New York Amsterdam News, February 27, 1965, p. 47.

689. "Malcolm Was Going to Miss.," New York Amsterdam News, February 27, 1965, p. 47.

690. "Malcolm Will Get Islamic Burial," New York Amsterdam News, February 27, 1965, p. 1.

691. "Malcolm X," New York Amsterdam News, February 27, 1965, p. 9.

692. "Malcolm X Accepts Invitation to Speak in Englewood, N. J.," New York Times, August 6, 1962, p. 27.

"Malcolm X Will Not Address Rally in Englewood, N. J.," New York Times, August 8, 1962, p. 63.

693. "Malcolm X Act Weighted: Many Rights Leaders Cool to Bolter's Policies," Baltimore Sun, March 11, 1964, p. 5.

694. "Malcolm X Addresses Demonstrators at Board Headquarters," New York Times, May 17, 1964, p. 1.

695. "Malcolm X and CORE Leader Mrs. Harrington Are Critical of President Kennedy Approval of March," New York Times, August 11, 1963, p. 1.

696. "Malcolm X and Other Modern Heroes Subjects of Biographies," Carolina Times, May 21, 1970, p. 5.

697. "Malcolm X Article Favors Goldwater," New York Times, September 8, 1964, p. 146.

698. "Malcolm X Assumes Leadership of Black Muslim Movement," New York Times, May 10, 1963, p. 1.

699. "Malcolm X at Harlem, NYC Rally to Support (Miss.) Freedom Democratic Party's Challenge to Seating 5 Representatives," New York Times, December 21, 1964, p. 20.

700. "Malcolm X Attacks Kennedy's Handling of Crisis (in Birmingham, Ala.)," New York Times, May 17, 1963, p. 14.

701. "Malcolm X Attacks U. S.," New York Times, August 23, 1964, p. 137.

702. "Malcolm X Backs Boycott While Opposing Its Aims," New York Times, March 16, 1964, p. 1.

703. "Malcolm X Backs House Rights Bills," New York Times, March 27, 1964, p. 50.

704. "Malcolm X Barred from Muslim's Chicago Convention," New York Amsterdam News, February 15, 1964, p. 1.

705. "Malcolm X Blames Johnson Support of Tshombe's Mercenaries for Killing of Hostages," New York Times, November 25, 1964, p. 17.

706. "Malcolm X Blames 'Scare Tactics' of Cops for Outbreak," World-Telegram, July 20, 1964.

707. "Malcolm X Buried in Femcliff Cemetery, Hartsdale, N. Y., Plot 150," New York Amsterdam News, March 13, 1965, p. 4.

708. "Malcolm X Calls for Muslim Peace," New York Times, June 27, 1964.

709. "Malcolm X Calls for Negro Unity," New York Amsterdam News (Brooklyn Edition), August 10, 1963.

710. "Malcolm X Case Is Reopened," Winston-Salem (N.C.) Journal, December 7, 1977.

711. "Malcolm X Changes Name to Malik Al Shabazz," Afro-American, December 5, 1964, p. 1.

712. "Malcolm X Charges President Fails to Aid Negroes, at Harlem Rally," New York Times, June 30, 1063, p. 45.

713. "Malcolm X (College) Picked for Educational Pilot," Chicago Daily Defender, March 20, 1971, p. 9.

714. "Malcolm X 'Comeback' In March," New York Amsterdam News, February 22, 1964, pp. 1, 2.

715. "Malcolm X Comments on BBC Coverage of His Trip in England," New York Times, February 14, 1965, p. 24.

716. "Malcolm X Denies Sect Pelted (Martin Luther) King," New York Post, July 1, 1963.

717. "Malcolm X Endorses Boycott," New York Amsterdam News (Brooklyn Edition), December 7, 1963.

718. "Malcolm X Feels 'At Home' in (Accra, Ghana) Africa," New York Times, May 13, 1964, p. 17.

719. "Malcolm X Flees for Life; Muslim Factions at War," New York Amsterdam News, June 20, 1964, pp. 1, 2.

720. "Malcolm X Few People Remember," Carolina Times, February 21, 1970, p. 2-A.

721. "Malcolm X Helped Stranded Workers," New York Amsterdam News, February 27, 1965, p. 25.

722. "Malcolm X in Eyes of Nation," New York Amsterdam News, April 27, 1963, pp. 1, 2.

723. "Malcolm X, In Apparent Criticism of Rep. A. C. Powell, Jr., Calls Him 'Flexible', Radio Interview," New York Times, June 10, 1963, p. 20.

724. "Malcolm X, in Cairo, Says He'll See African Leaders," New York Times, July 14, 1964, p. 23.

725. "Malcolm X, in Traffic Court, Denies Speeding on Bridge," New York Times, March 17, 1964, p. 18.

726. "Malcolm X Is Black Hero, A Black Symbol, A Black Concept," New York Courier, May 22, 1971, pp. 1, 2, 5, 20.

727. "Malcolm X Is No Longer Angriest Muslim of All," Journal and Guide, July 18, 1964, p. 14.

728. "Malcolm X Is Observer (at NAACP Convention)," New York Times, June 27, 1964, p. 10.

729. "Malcolm X Lays Harlem Riot to 'Scare Tactics' of Police," New York Times, July 21, 1964, p. 121.

730. "Malcolm X--Many Things to Many People," New York Amsterdam News, February 27, 1965, p. 7.

731. "Malcolm X May Be Replaced as Minister of Mosque 7 in New York City," New York Times, December 6, 1963, p. 27.

732. "Malcolm X Murder Is Unsolved," New York Amsterdam News, July 31, 1965, p. 1.

733. "Malcolm X Murder Trial," New York Amsterdam News, February 5, 1966, p. 1.

734. "Malcolm X Not Being Viewed As Martyr Even in Asian and African Nations," New York Times, February 28, 1965, p. 74.

735. "Malcolm X on Payne August 4th Article on Islam and Contrasting Black Muslim Movement; Payne Replies," New York Times, August 25, 1963, p. 2, Section VI.

736. "Malcolm X on Plans for Services at Muslim Mosque, Inc.," New York Times, March 23, 1964, p. 18.

737. "Malcolm X on the 'Trap of Racism'," Sacramento Observer, May 18, 1972, p. A-7.

738. "Malcolm X Refers to President Kennedy Assassination as 'Chickens Coming Home to Roost'," New York Times, December 2, 1963, p. 21.

739. "Malcolm X Reports He Now Represents World Muslim Body," New York Times, October 11, 1964.

740. "Malcolm X Returns to U.S.," New York Times, November 25, 1964, p. 17.

741. "Malcolm X, Rev. Galamison, Rep. A. C. Powell, Jr., Appear at Rally (in Brooklyn, N.Y.)," New York Times, May 17, 1964, p. 25.

742. "Malcolm X Says Peace a Miracle," Afro-American, May 30, 1964, p. 1.

743. "Malcolm X Sees New Light in Mecca Visit," Afro-American, May 16, 1964, p. 12.

744. "Malcolm X Supporter Wins Release on Bail," The Militant, March 22, 1965, p. 8.

745. "Malcolm X Tells of Death Threat," New York Amsterdam News, March 24, 1964, p. 1.

746. "Malcolm X to Address N. Y. Forum," The Militant, December 21, 1964, p. 8.

747. "Malcolm X to Meet Leaders of Africa," New York Times, July 10, 1964, p. 26.

748. "The Malcolm X Trial, 'The Limit' Is Sought," New York Amsterdam News, December 14, 1965, p. 51.

749. "Malcolm X Trial to Jury," New York Amsterdam News, March 12, 1966, p. 3.

750. "Malcolm X Trial for 3 Scheduled," New York Amsterdam News, November 20, 1965, p. 1.

751. "Malcolm X Trial 2nd Week," New York Amsterdam News, January 29, 1966, p. 1.

752. "Malcolm X Trial Setting Precedents," New York Amsterdam News, February 12, 1966, p. 1.

753. "Malcolm X Urges Negroes to Join His Black Nationalist Organization," New York Times, March 23, 1964, p. 18.

754. "Malcolm X Was a Black Man," The Black Panther, May 19, 1970, pp. 10-11.

Article states that it is the thoughts of Huey P. Newton underscored by the ideology and philosophy seeded by Malcolm X that holds the Black Panther Party together and constitutes its foundation.

755. "Malcolm X: Why I Quit and What I Plan Next: His Resignation Stirs Muhammad," New York Amsterdam News, March 14, 1964, p. 1.

756. "Malcolm X Widow Gets $500 Gift (from Mrs. W. E. B. DuBois)," New York Amsterdam News, March 20, 1965, p. 26.

757. "Malcolm's Aide Dies in Mystery," New York Amsterdam News, March 20, 1965, p. 39.

758. "Malcolm's Funeral Services," New York Amsterdam News, February 27, 1965, p. 1.

759. "Malcolm's Gun Idea Gets Cool Response," Afro-American, March 28, 1964, p. 11.

760. "Malcolm X's Letter (Re: Jackie Robinson)," New York Amsterdam News, November 30, 1963, pp. 2, 3.

761. "Malcolm X's Widow to Lecture on Him," New York Amsterdam News, February 22, 1969, pp. 1, 34.

762. "Malcolm X's Widow Will Miss Trial-Lawyers Named," New York Amsterdam News, December 11, 1965, p. 1.

763. "Man on Trial for Malcolm X Murder Tells Court He Took Part in Crime," Washington Post, March 1, 1966.

764. "Markings on Malcolm's Grave," New York Amsterdam News, March 13, 1965, p. 4.

765. Marsh, Trenna. "Another Look at Malcolm X," Michigan Chronicle, March 28, 1970, p. 11.

766. "Martin Luther King and Roy Wilkins: On Malcolm's Death," New York Amsterdam News, February 27, 1965, p. 27.

767. Matthews, Les. "Malcolm X Killer Talks; Names 4," New York Amsterdam News, April 29, 1978, p. 1.

768. ______________. "Malcolm X Murder Is Unsolved," New York Amsterdam News, July 31, 1965.

769. ______________. "Malcolm X Questions L.B.J.," New York Amsterdam News, May 30, 1964.

770. McGill, Ralph. "Essay on Malcolm X and Black Muslims," Detroit News, March 3, 1965.

771. McManus, Jane. "The Outlook of Malcolm X," National Guardian, April 18, 1964.

772. Miller, Roland. "Malcolm X: The Final Interview," Flamingo (Ghana Edition), June, 1965.

773. Montgomery, Paul L. "Malcolm X, A Harlem Idol on Eve of Murder Trial," New York Times, December 6, 1965.

774. "Mothers Raising Cash for Malcolm X's Family," New York Amsterdam News, March 20, 1965, p. 30.

775. "Mrs. E. Collins Says She Has Taken Over As Afro-American Unity Organization Chairman, Succeeding Malcolm X," New York Times, March 16, 1965, p. 33.

776. "Mrs. Malcolm X Fund Now at $4,000," New York Amsterdam News, March 6, 1965, p. 2.

777. "Muslim Minister Blasts Malcolm X," New York Amsterdam News, January 30, 1965, p. 6.

778. "Muslim Talk Approved: New York City College President Clears Appearance by Malcolm X," New York Times, November 23, 1961, p. 50.

779. "Nationalist Plead for Malcolm X," New York Amsterdam News, February 29, 1964, p. 1.

780. "Nearly 2,000 Negroes Hear Malcolm X Speak in Detroit," The Militant, April 20, 1964, p. 8.

781. "Negro Moderation Decried by Malcolm X in Lebanon," New York Times, May 2, 1964, p. 79.

782. "Negro Rule Predicted by Muslim," Greensboro Daily News, January 31, 1963, p. 1.

Malcolm X spoke to Blacks at J. C. Smith University in Charlotte, NC.

783. "Negroes Won't Start Violence, Black Muslim Leader Predicts," World-Telegram, March 10, 1964.

784. "New Manhattan Borough President (Constance) Motley Says Malcolm X Death Affords New York City Opportunity to Lead Negroes Into 'Constructive Channels of Activity'," World-Telegram, March 1, 1965, p. 17.

785. "New Malcolm X Center Offers Hope," The Philadelphia Tribune, February 23, 1982, pp. 1, 18.

786. "No 'Cheek Turning' Says Malcolm X," New York Amsterdam News, July 4, 1964, p. 48.

787. Norden, Eric. "Who Killed Malcolm X?," The Realist, February, 1967.

788. "N. Y. Leader Malcolm X Seen in Power Struggle with Leaders around Elijah Muhammed," New York Times, February 26, 1964, p. 39.

789. Paris, Martin. "Negroes Are Willing to Use Terrorism, Says Malcolm X," Columbia Daily Spectator, February 19, 1965.

790. "P. B. Zuber Invites Black Muslim Leader Malcolm X to Attend Anti-Segregation Rally in Englewood, New Jersey," New York Times, August 5, 1962, p. 55.

791. Phillips, Waldo B. "Political Implications of Malcolm X's Death," Los Angeles Herald Dispatch, March 4, 1965.

792. "Playwright Discusses the Death of Malcolm X," New York Amsterdam News, February 27, 1965, p. 16.

793. Poinsett, Alex. "Dr. Charles G. Hurst-Mastermind of Malcolm X College," Ebony, March, 1970, pp. 29-38.

794. "Police Force at Clay-Liston Bout to Be Tripled Because of Reports that Malcolm X Followers May Try to Kill Clay," New York Times, May 21, 1965, p. 24.

795. Porter, Herman. "Postpone Trial of Three in Malcolm X Murder Until Beginning of Year," The Militant, December 13, 1965, p. 8.

796. Porter, Ruth. "Paris Meeting Hears Malcolm X," The Militant, December 7, 1964, p. 4.

797. Poston, Tom. "Clay in Malcolm X's Corner in Black Muslim Power Fight," New York Post, March 1, 1964.

798. "Postpone Malcolm X Home Case," New York Amsterdam News, April 25, 1964.

799. Powledge, Fred. "Negroes Ponder Malcolm's Move: Differ Over Significance of His Political Effort," New York Times, March 15, 1964.

800. Prattis, P. L. "Malcolm X Trying to Make Racket Out of Desperation," Michigan Chronicle, March 28, 1964, p. 1.

801. Price, William A. "Malcolm's Death Spotlights Gap Between Negro and White," National Guardian, March 6, 1965.

802. ________________. "Negro Marches Ask 'Black Power'," National Guardian, June 25, 1966.

803. "Princeton Sociologist Analyzes the Muslims," New York Amsterdam News (Brooklyn Edition), February 8, 1964.

804. "Prosecution Rests in Malcolm X (Murder) Case," New York Times, February 19, 1966, p. 21.

805. "Protect Malcolm X Jurors," New York Amsterdam News, January 22, 1966, p. 1.

806. Protz, Roger. "Millions of Britons See Malcolm X in TV Broadcast of Debate at Oxford," The Militant, December 14, 1964, p. 2.

807. "Queens (College) Dean Bans Talk by (Malcolm X) Black Muslim," New York Post, October 18, 1961.

808. "Quotations of Malcolm X," Sacramento Observer, May 21, 1970, p. 10.

809. "Real Malcolm X," New York Amsterdam News, March 20, 1965, p. 34.

810. "A Reconstruction of Malcolm X's Personality," Afro-American, June, 1972, pp. 1-6.

811. "Reply to Malcolm X August 25th Article on Black Muslim Teachings," New York Times, September 25, 1963, p. 40, Section VI.

812. "Report that Black Muslim Leader Malcolm X is Moving from New York City to Washington, D. C.," New York Times, May 6, 1963, p. 59.

813. "Rev. A. D. King and Malcolm X Address Rally in Harlem to Aid Birmingham Blacks," New York Times, May 15, 1963, p. 26.

814. Ring, Harry. "New York Cops Harass Malcolm X Supporters," The Militant, April 5, 1965, p. 1.

815. Robinson, Jackie. "Bullets Silenced a Man of Courage," Michigan Chronicle, March 13, 1965.

816. ________. "Jackie Robinson Again Writes to Malcolm X," New York Amsterdam News, December 14, 1963, pp. 1, 53.

817. "...Role of Black Muslims and Malcolm X Discussed (in Article on 'Black Nationalism')," New York Times, April 23, 1963, p. 20.

818. Roth, Jack. "3 Get Life Terms in Malcolm Case," New York Times, April 15, 1966, p. 36.

819. "Roy Wilkins Says Malcolm X Has Not 'Stirred' Anybody Except N.Y. Times," New York Times, June 21, 1963, p. 14.

820. "San Francisco Symposium on Malcolm Book: George Novack and Eldridge Speak," The Militant, May 22, 1967, p. 6.

821. Schaap, Dick. "The Paradox That Is Malcolm X: All Charm and All Contradiction," New York Herald Tribune, March 22, 1964, p. 28.

822. "See Early Trial on Malcolm," New York Amsterdam News, August 21, 1965, p. 1.

823. "Seek to Evict Malcolm X from Home in Queens," New York Amsterdam News, April 18, 1964, p. 1.

824. "Seek to Link Malcolm X to Slayings in Harlem: Queens DA Cites Malcolm's Speech," New York Amsterdam News, May 9, 1964, p. 1.

825. Smith, Ed. "Report October Trial Set in Killing of Malcolm X," The Militant, October 4, 1965, p. 1.

826. Solet, Sue. "Malcolm X on a Mission," New York Herald Tribune, May 5, 1963.

827. "Somebody Was After Malcolm X," New York Amsterdam News, February 27, 1965, p. 19.

828. "The Speech Malcolm Wanted to Make," New York Amsterdam News, February 27, 1965, p. 47.

829. Spellman, A. B. "Malcolm X vs. James Farmer: Separation vs. Integration. Debate," Dialogue Magazine, 1962.

830. Spiegel, Irving. "6 Black Nationalists Indicted as Result of Clash in Harlem," New York Times, July 4, 1964, p. 101.

831. "Stars to Raise Funds for Mrs. Malcolm X," New York Amsterdam News, April 17, 1965, p. 49.

832. "Statement on Malcolm X's Murder," West Africa, February 27, 1965, p. 246.

833. Stone, I. J. "The Pilgrimage of Malcolm X," New York Review of Books, November 11, 1965.

834. Storey, Robert. "Goodbye, Booker T.," Beacon Magazine (Emerson College), Spring, 1970, p. 18.

Author surmised that Malcolm's ideas converted the intellectual and biracial civil rights movement into a "struggle for identity' for the Black masses.

835. "Supporter of Malcolm X Faces Police Frame-Up," The Militant, March 8, 1965, p. 1.

836. "$13,000 to Malcolm's Widow," New York Amsterdam News, May 29, 1965, p. 1.

837. "3 Get Life Terms in Malcolm X Case," The Militant, April 25, 1969, p. 2.

838. "3 Who Murder Malcolm X Given Life Terms," Jet, April 28, 1966, p. 27.

839. "Thomas Hagan, Talma 15X Johnson, and Norman 3X Butler, Brought to Trial for Malcolm X Slaying," New York Amsterdam News, January 22, 1966, p. 1.

840. "Threats of Violence Reported Directed Against Malcolm X," The Militant, June 22, 1964, p. 8.

841. Todd, George. "Malcolm X Explains His Rifle Statement," New York Amsterdam News, March 28, 1964, p. 1.

842. "20 Gather to Listen to Voice of Malcolm X," Washington Post, June 18, 1967, p. E-50.

843. "Twins Born to Mrs. Malcolm X," New York Amsterdam News, October 9, 1965, p. 1.

844. Ubahakwe, E. Ebo. "Nigerian View of Malcolm," The Militant, April 5, 1965, p. 7.

845. Wallace, Mike, and Louis Lomax. "The Hate That Hate Produced," Newsbeat (New York), WNTA-TV (July 10, 1958) television program.

846. "Warner Bros. to Film Malcolm X's Autobiography," New York Amsterdam News, January 23, 1971, p. 1.

847. "Warrant for Malcolm as Speeder is Issued," New York Times, May 20, 1964, p. 33.

848. "Watch Kept in New York and Chicago: Suspect is Held in Slaying of Negro Leader," Washington Evening Star, February 22, 1965, pp. A-1, 3.

849. Weber, Shirley N. "Black Nationalism and Garveyist Influences," Western Journal of Black Studies, Vol. 3, No. 4, Winter, 1979. Malcolm X pp. 263, 266.

850. Wechsler, James A. "About Malcolm X," New York Post, February 23, 1965.

851. ________________. "What Killed Malcolm X," Weekly People, March 13, 1965.

852. West, Hollie I. "'Malcolm X': Manhood, a Documentary Film," Washington Post, May 23, 1967, pp. B-1, B-6.

853. "What Harlemites Say About Malcolm X Slaying," New York Amsterdam News, February 27, 1965, p. 22.

854. "What Malcolm X Really Stood For," The Militant, March 1, 1965, p. 5.

855. White, Robert. "The Feud That Led to Death (of Malcolm X)," New York Herald Tribune, February 22, 1965, p. 1.

856. "Whites, Hypocrites Love Malcolm," Muhammad Speaks, October 3, 1969, pp. 20-21.

857. "Who Sent 10G Check to Malcolm X Slaying Suspect?," New York Amsterdam News, March 13, 1965, p. 1.

858. Wilkins, Roy. "Malcolm X-ism Jars White Complacency," Detroit News, January 3, 1965.

859. ___________. "No Time for Avengers," New York Amsterdam News, March 6, 1965.

860. ___________. "The Repercussions of Malcolm X's Death," Detroit News, March 7, 1965.

861. Williams, Robert F. "The Crusader and Mr. Elijah Muhammad," The Crusader, May, 1963.

862. ___________. "Malcolm X: Death Without Silence," The Crusader, March, 1965.

863. Wilson, C. E. "Without Malcolm X," Economist, Vol. 214, February 27, 1965, p. 888.

864. Wooten, James. "Malcolm X University to Open in Durham (N.C.) as Militants' School," New York Times, October 28, 1969, p. 48.

865. Worthy, William. "After the Break with Muhammad Malcolm X Says Group Will Stress Politics," National Guardian, March 21, 1964, p. 4.

866. ___________. "X on the Spot," Newsweek, Vol. 62, No. 25, December 16, 1963, pp. 27-28.

867. Young, Whitney Jr. "Malcolm's Death Solves Nothing," New York World-Telegram and Sun, February 25, 1965.

APPENDIXES

A
Dissertations and Theses

1. MAJOR WORKS

868. Anderson, Kay E. "A Study of Theme in Autobiographical Works of Claude Brown, Dick Gregory, Malcolm X, and Richard Wright, with Emphasis on the Autobiographical Writings of James Baldwin." Unpublished Master's Thesis, Whittier College, 1971.

869. Harper, Frederick D. "Maslow's Concept of Self-Actualization Compared with Personality Charactertistics of Selected Black American Protesters: Martin Luther King, Jr., Malcolm X and Frederick Douglass." Unpublished Doctoral Dissertation, Florida State University, 1970. 167 pp.

870. Luellen, David E. "Ministers and Martyrs: Malcolm X and Martin Luther King, Jr." Unpublished Doctoral Dissertation, Ball State University, 1972. 263 pp.

871. McGuire, Robert Grayson III. "Continuity in Black Political Protest: The Thoughts of Booker T. Washington, W. E. B. DuBois, Marcus Garvey, Malcolm X, Joseph Casely Hayford, Joseph B. Dangnah, and Kwame Nkrumah. Unpublished Doctoral Dissertation, Columbia University, 1974. 321 pp.

872. Onwubu, Chukwuemeka. "Black Ideologies and the Sociology of Knowledge: The Public Response to the Protest Thoughts and Teaching of Martin Luther King, Jr. and Malcolm X." Unpublished Doctoral Dissertation, Michigan State University, 1975. 202 pp.

873. Payne, James Chris II. "A Content Analysis of Speeches and Written Documents of Six Black Spokesmen: Frederick Douglass, W. E. B. DuBois, Martin Luther King, Jr. and Malcolm X." Unpublished Doctoral Dissertation, Florida State University, 1970. 126 pp.

874. Rydzka-Ostyn, Brygida Irena. "The Oratory of Martin Luther King and Malcolm X: A Study in Linguistic Stylistics." Unpublished Doctoral Dissertation, University of Rochester, 1972. 187 pp.

875. Wood, James C. "Humor as a Form of Political Action: The Case of Malcolm X." Unpublished Doctoral Dissertation, Arizona State University, 1975. 293 pp.

2. GENERAL WORKS

A Selected List

876. Nelson, Ausbrooks Beth. "Muslims, Militants, Moderates: A Comparative Analysis on Concepts of Black Power." Unpublished Doctoral Dissertation, Howard University, 1971. "Malcolm X," pp. 84-85, 101-108, 128.

Writer declares that many of the general white society, as well as many Black Americans, took what Malcolm said of discrimination and the Black American's roots in slavery to mean Black against white.

877. Shelton, Robert L. "Black Revolution: The Definition and Meaning of 'Revolution' in the Writings and Speeches of Selected Nationally Prominent Negro Americans, 1963-1968." Unpublished Doctoral Dissertation, Boston University, 1970. 428 pp.

878. Tyler, Lawrence L. "The Black Muslim Identity as Viewed by Non-Muslim Blacks." Unpublished Doctoral Dissertation, University of Missouri-Columbia, 1970. "Malcolm X," pp. 9, 24, 25, 51, 55, 56.

Writer compares and contrasts Eldridge Cleaver's life with that of Malcolm X.

B
Obituaries, Memorials, Tributes, and Honors

A Selected List

879. "About 1,000 Negroes Mark Birthday of Late Malcolm X with March through Bedford-Stuyvesant Section," New York Times, May 20, 1968, p. 50.

880. "About 600 Negroes Attend Memorial Services for Malcolm X at IS 201," New York Times, February 22, 1968, p. 1.

881. Alexander, Mike. "In Tribute to our Black Prince, Malcolm X," The Hilltop, February 21, 1975, p. 8.

882. "Black Muslims Assault the People at Malcolm X Festival Held at Philadelphia Community College," The Black Panther, March 7, 1970, pp. 7, 16.

883. "Blacks March (in Durham, N. C.), Honor Malcolm X," Durham Morning Herald, May 20, 1970, p. 2.

884. "Baldwin: Malcolm's Death Is a 'Setback'," New York Amsterdam News, February 27, 1965, p. 20.

885. Booker, James. "Malcolm X: Why I Quit (Nation of Islam) and What I Plan Next; His Resignation Stuns (Elijah) Muhammad," New York Amsterdam News, March 14, 1964, pp. 1, 51.

886. Buder, Leonard. "Donovan Yelds on IS 201 Event: Malcolm X Memorial To Be Held this Morning," New York Times, February 21, 1968, p. 33.

887. ______________. "Program Honoring Malcolm X in East Harlem School Barred," New York Times, February 17, 1968, p. 18.

888. "Buffalo (N.Y.) Players Pay Tribute to Malcolm X," Contrast (Toronto, Canada), May 1, 1981, p. 18.

889. "Camejo in Speech About Malcolm X (at Berkeley (CA) High School)," The Militant, March 6, 1967, p. 8.

890. Dash, Leon. "Memory of Malcolm X Honored at AU (American University)," Washington Post, February 22, 1968.

891. Davis, George. "Plans Set to Honor Malcolm X," Washington Post, May 4, 1969.

892. Dumoulin, Henri. "African Reactions to Malcolm X's Death: Report from Algeria," The Militant, March 29, 1965, p. 6.

893. Editorial. "A Tribute to Black Prince: Malcolm X," New York Amsterdam News, February 19, 1972, p. 2-A.

894. Editorial. "Hate: Full Circle," New York Herald Tribune, February 23, 1965.

895. Editorial. "Malcolm X Day: May 19," New York Amsterdam News, May 20, 1978, p. A-4.

896. "El Hajj Malik Shabazz (Malcolm X): May 19, 1925-Feb. 21, 1965," News and Letter (Institute of Race Relations), March, 1965, pp. 16-19.

897. "Few Stores in D. C. Honor Malcolm X," Washington Post, May 21, 1968.

898. "4 Day Celebration Marks Malcolm X," New York Amsterdam News, May 16, 1970, pp. 1, 47.

899. Geller, Lawrence H. "Students (Parkway School in Philadelphia) Mark Birthdays of Malcolm X and Ho Chi Minh," Philadelphia Tribune, May 22, 1071, p. 12.

900. "Honoring King, Malcolm X," Washington Post, February 2, 1974.

901. "Honoring Malcolm's Birthday OAAU Calls for 'Drums' May 19th," New York Amsterdam News, May 20, 1978, p. 1.

902. "In Memory of Malcolm X," New York Amsterdam News, May 19, 1973, pp. A-1, A-2.

903. "Indonesian Students Demonstrating at Jakarta Residence of United States Ambassador Jones, Say they Are Protesting Slaying of Malcolm X," New York Times, March 1, 1965, p. 4.

904. Johnson, Thomas. "March in Harlen Honors Malcolm X," New York Times, February 23, 1967, p. 26.

905. Jones, Deborah. "Malcolm X Tribute on Friday," Tech News (N. Y. City College), Vol. 31, No. 3, February 17 1970, p. 222.

906. Lerner, Max. "Malcolm's Death," New York Post, February 26, 1965.

907. "Letters to the Editor on Malcolm X's Death," The Militant, March 22, 1965, p. 7.

908. Lewis, Alfred. "Store Closings Asked as Malcolm X Tribute," Washington Post, May 17, 1968.

909. "Life of Malcolm X Receives Homage (as Thousands Commemorate His 45th Birthday)," Daily World, May 19, 1970.

910. "Malcolm X," New York Times, February 22, 1965.

911. "Malcolm X Day (Celebration)," Sacramento Observer, May 22, 1969, pp. 9, 10.

912. "Malcolm X Day Parade Set Sat.," New York Amsterdam News, February 21, 1970, p. 42.

913. "(Malcolm X) Death of a Desperado," Newsweek, March 8, 1965, pp. 24-25.

914. "(Malcolm X) Died as John Doe," New York Amsterdam News, February 27, 1965, p. 6.

915. "Malcolm X Memorial," Muntu Drum (Cuyahoga Community College, Cleveland, Ohio), February 27, 1973, p. 1.

916. "Malcolm X Memorial-1969," Black Theatre, April, 1970, pp. 39-40.

917. "Malcolm X Memorial at IS 201," New York Amsterdam News, February 17, 1968, p. 3.

918. "Malcolm X Memorial Program at Audubon Ballroom in Harlem, N. Y., February 21, 1978," Black Star, March, 1978, pp. 1, 7.

919. "Malcolm X Memory Perpetuates," New York Amsterdam News, May 23, 1970, p. 2.

920. "Malcolm X Parade, Sunday," New York Amsterdam News, May 18, 1968, p. 23.

921. "Malcolm X Day Set May 19," New York Amsterdam News, April 23, 1966, Section B, p. 9.

922. "Malcolm X To Be Honored On Day of Assassination Feb. 21st. in East," New York Amsterdam News, February 15, 1975.

923. "Malcolm X Tributes," The Militant, May 29, 1967, p. 8.

924. "Malcolm's Birthday Tribute," New York Amsterdam News, May 25, 1968, p. 25.

925. "Many Memorial Meetings Around Nation Pay Tribute to Memory of Malcolm X," The Militant, March 6, 1967, p. 4.

926. "Marking Birthday of Malcolm-Scholarship Fund Set Up," New York Amsterdam News, May 17, 1969, p. 3.

927. Marsh, Jack. "Chicago Memorial Meeting Aids Family of Malcolm X," The Militant, April 19, 1965, p. 2.

928. "Meeting in Harlem Honors Malcolm X," The Militant, June 7, 1965, p. 8.

929. "Memorial Held in Malcolm X's Honor May 19th," New York Age, May 25, 1974.

930. "Memorial Program Feb. 21, 1979, is 14th Anniversary of the Killing of Malcolm X, to be Held at Boys and Girls High School Auditorium, Brooklyn, N. Y.," New York Daily Challenge, February 14, 1979, p. 5.

931. "Memorials to Malcolm X Slated by Three Forums," The Militant, February 13, 1967, p. 1.

932. "Milwaukee Civil Rights Forces Join in Memorial Meeting for Malcolm X," The Militant, May 17, 1965, p. 8.

933. "Nation of Islam's Harlem, N.Y.C. Mosque Named for Malcolm X Shabazz," Jet, February 19, 1976, p. 10.

934. "Negro Pupils Extend Tribute to Malcolm X," Washington Evening Star, February 22, 1969.

935. "OAAU Harlem Rally Marks 'Malcolm X Memorial Day'," The Militant, May 31, 1965, p. 5.

936. "OAAU (Organization of Afro-American Unity) Plans 3-Day Malcolm X Honors," New York Amsterdam News, May 10, 1969, p. 12.

937. "Ossie Davis in Tribute to Malcolm X," New York Amsterdam News, February 26, 1966, p. 1.

938. "Ossie Davis' Stirring Tribute to Malcolm X," New York Amsterdam News, March 6, 1965, p. 1.

939. "Pilgrimage to Malcolm X Grave (Ferncliff Cemetery, Hartsdale, N.Y.) Marks Beginning of Week-Long Birthday Celebration," New York Amsterdam News, May 20, 1972, p. A-1.

940. "Plan Memorial Honoring 10th Anniversary of His (Malcolm X) Assassination Feb. 21, 1975-The East is Sponsoring the Meeting at IS 201 in Harlem, N.Y.," New York Daily Challenge, February 18, 1975, p. 2.

941. "A Prayer to El Hajj Malik (Malcolm X)," The Black Panther, May 19, 1970, p. 18.

942. Price, William A. "Malcolm's Death Spotlights Gap Between Negro and White," National Guardian, March 6, 1965.

943. "Reactions to Death of Malcolm X," The Militant, March 1, 1965, p. 4.

944. "Remember Malcolm X's Birthday," New York Amsterdam News, May 23, 1970, pp. 1, 3.

945. "Remember the Words of Brother Malcolm: Pay Homage to Brother Malcolm on May 19-20, Do Not Go to Work, Do Not Go to School," The Black Panther, May 18, 1968, pp. 6, 7.

946. "Rev. Cleage Remembers Malcolm X on Natal Day," Baltimore Afro-American, May 23, 1970, p. 2.

947. Robeson, Eslanda. "Malcolm X's Funeral, Dignity and Brotherhood," Baltimore Afro-American, March 20, 1965.

948. "Services in Indonesia for Malcolm X," The Militant, March 29, 1965, p. 6.

949. "75 March to Mark Malcolm's Death," New York Times, February 21, 1966, p. 45.

950. Shabazz, James. "Weep for Brother Malcolm, He Is Dead," The Militant, March 15, 1965.

951. "'Speak Out'. Youth Outspoken in TV Discussion of 'Heroes'(Malcolm X Is One)," New York Amsterdam News, November 20, 1965, p. 13.

952. "Speakers at the Militant Labor Forum Memorial Meeting Pay Tribute to Malcolm X," The Militant, March 15, 1965, pp. 1, 3.

953. "Speakers (James Shabazz, Farrell Dobbs, Robert Vernon, Jack Barnes) Pay Tribute to Malcolm X," The Militant, March 15, 1965, p. 1.

954. "State New York Benefit for Malcolm X's Family," The Militant, March 29, 1965, p. 6.

955. "Story of Malcolm and Elijah Aired," Los Angeles Sentinel, February 18, 1982, p. B-7.

956. Strickland, William L. "Epitaph on Malcolm X," NSM: Freedom North, Vol. 1, No. 3, 1965, pp. 1, 17.

957. "The Prince of Black Dignity: Malcolm X, 1925-1965," Sacramento Observer, May 20, 1971, p. A-9.

958. "Thousands Attend Rites for Malcolm X," Washington Sunday Star, February 28, 1965, p. B-4.

959. "Tribute to a Black Man," New York Amsterdam News, March 20, 1965, p. 34.

960. "30,000 Mourn Malcolm X," New York Amsterdam News, March 6, 1965, p. 33.

961. "20 Gather to Listen to (Record) Voice of Malcolm X," Washington Post, June 18, 1967, p. E-50.

962. "200 Demonstrate in London Over Murder of Malcolm X," The Militant, March 29, 1965, p. 6.

963. "Universal Islamic Brotherhood Confab to Commemorate Malcolm X," The Call and Post (Cleveland), February 20, 1982, p. 7-B.

964. "When Malcolm Died," New York Amsterdam News, February 19, 1966, p. 1.

965. White, Butch. "Remembrance: Malcolm X," Black World, Vol. 24, No. 7, May, 1975, pp. 88-89.

966. "Young Socialists Send Message (to Malcolm X's Widow, Betty Shabazz)," The Militant, March 1, 1965, p. 4.

C
Poetry Inspired by Malcolm X

A Selected List

967. Alba, Nanina. "For Malcolm," *For Malcolm X: Poems on the Life and Death of Malcolm X*, Dudley Randall and Margaret G. Burroughs, Editors. Detroit: Broadside Press, 1969, p. 39.

968. Allen, Ernie. "For Malcolm," *Soulbook*, Vol. 1, No. 2, Spring, 1965, pp. 85-86.

969. Augustin, Elisabeth. *Het Onvoltooide Leven Van Malcolm X*. Amsterdam: n.p. 1973.

970. Barrax, Gerald W. "For Malcolm: After Mecca," *Celebrations: A New Anthology of Black American Poetry*, Arnold Adoff, Editor. Chicago: Follett Publishing Co., 1977, p. 184.

971. Brooks, Gwendolyn. "Malcolm X," *Celebrations: A New Anthology of Black American Poetry*, Arnold Adoff, Editor. Chicago: Follett Publishing Co., 1977, p. 181.

972. _________________. "Malcolm X," *In The Mecca*. New York: Harper & Row, 1967.

973. _________________. "Malcolm X," *For Malcolm X: Poems on the Life and Death of Malcolm X*, Dudley Randall and Margaret G. Burroughs, Editors. Detroit: Broadside Press, 1969, p. 3.

974. Burroughs, Margaret. "Brother Freedom," *For Malcolm X: Poems on the Life and Death of Malcolm X*, Dudley Randall and Margaret G. Burroughs, Editors. Detroit: Broadside Press, 1969, p. 22.

975. Caine, Maecella. "Jungle Flower," *For Malcolm X: Poems on the Life and Death of Malcolm X*, Dudley Randall and Margaret G. Burroughs, Editors. Detroit: Broadside Press, 1969, p. 8.

976. Clifton, Lucille. "Malcolm," *Celebrations: A New Anthology of Black American Poetry*, Arnold Adoff, Editor. Chicago: Follett Publishing Co., 1977, p. 180.

977. Cumbo, Kattie M. "Malcolm," *Black Out Loud*, Arnold Adoff, Editor. New York: Dell Publishing Co., 1970, p. 56.

978. Danner, Margaret. "Malcolm X, A Lover of the Grass Roots," *For Malcolm X: Poems on the Life and Death of Malcolm X*, Dudley Randall and Margaret G. Burroughs, Editors. Detroit: Broadside Press, 1969, p. 6.

979. David, Llorens. "One Year Ago," *A Broadside Treasury*, Gwendolyn Brooks, Editor. Detroit: Broadside Press, 1971, p. 22.

980. Evans, Mari. "The Insurgent," *For Malcolm X: Poems on the Life and Death of Malcolm X*, Dudley Randall and Margaret G. Burroughs, Editors. Detroit: Broadside Press, 1969, p. 4.

981. Fields, Julia. "Aardvark," *Celebrations: A New Anthology of Black American Poetry*, Arnold Adoff, Editor. Chicago: Follett Publishing Co., 1977, p. 182.

982. ______________. "For Malcolm X," *For Malcolm X: Poems on the Life and Death of Malcolm X*, Dudley Randall and Margaret G. Burroughs, Editors. Detroit: Broadside Press, 1969, p. 33.

983. Foreman, Kent. "Judgment Day: For Big Red, the Darwinian Doge, R.I.P.," *For Malcolm X: Poems on the Life and Death of Malcolm X*, Dudley Randall and Margaret G. Burroughs, Editors. Detroit: Broadside Press, 1969.

984. ______________. "Judgment Day," *A Broadside Treasury*, Gwendolyn Brooks, Editor. Detroit: Broadside Press, 1971, p. 26.

985. Frederick, Bill. "Malcolm," *For Malcolm X: Poems on the Life and Death of Malcolm X*, Dudley Randall and Margaret G. Burroughs, Editors. Detroit: Broadside Press, 1969, p. 24.

986. Gilbert, Zack. "Written After Thinking of Malcolm," *For Malcolm X: Poems on the Life and Death of Malcolm X*, Dudley Randall and Margaret G. Burroughs, Editors. Detroit: Broadside Press, 1969, p. 72.

987. Goodwin, Leroy. "A Tribute to Malcolm X," *Liberator*, Vol. 8, No. 2, February, 1968, p. 13.

988. Goulbourne, Carmin Auld. "Letter for El-Hajj Malik El-Shabazz," *For Malcolm X: Poems on the Life and Death of Malcolm X*, Dudley Randall and Margaret G. Burroughs, Editors. Detroit: Broadside Press, 1969, p. 29.

989. Graham, Le. "The Black Shining Prince," *For Malcolm X: Poems on the Life and Death of Malcolm X*, Dudley Randall and Margaret G. Burroughs, Editors. Detroit: Broadside Press, 1969, p. 26.

990. Hamilton, Bobb. "For Malik," *For Malcolm X: Poems on the Life and Death of Malcolm X*, Dudley Randall and Margaret G. Burroughs, Editors. Detroit: Broadside Press, 1969, p. 43.

991. ______________. "Memorial Day," *For Malcolm X: Poems on the Life and Death of Malcolm X*, Dudley Randall and Margaret G. Burroughs, Editors. Detroit: Broadside Press, 1969, p. 80.

992. Hayden, Robert. "El-Hajj Malik El-Shabazz," *For Malcolm X: Poems on the Life and Death of Malcolm X*, Dudley Randall and Margaret G. Burroughs, Editors. Detroit: Broadside Press, 1969, p. 14.

993. ______________. "El-Hajj Malik El-Shabazz," *A Broadside Treasury*, Gwendolyn Brooks, Editor. Detroit: Broadside Press, 1971, pp. 20-21.

994. ______________. "El-Hajj Malik El-Shabazz (Malcolm X)," *Celebrations: A New Anthology of Black American Poetry*, Arnold Adoff, Editor. Chicago: Follett Publishing Co., 1977, pp. 184-186.

995. Henderson, David. "They Are Killing All The Young Men," *For Malcolm X: Poems on the Life and Death of Malcolm X*, Dudley Randall and Margaret G. Burroughs, Editors. Detroit: Broadside Press, 1969, p. 46.

996. Horne, Theodore R. "Malcolm Exsiccated," *Soulbook 2*, Vol. 1, No. 2, Spring, 1965, p. 124.

997. _________________. "Malcolm Exsiccated," *For Malcolm X: Poems on the Life and Death of Malcolm X*, Dudley Randall and Margaret G. Burroughs, Editors. Detroit: Broadside Press, 1969, p. 67.

998. _________________. "There's Fire," *For Malcolm X: Poems on the Life and Death of Malcolm X*, Dudley Randall and Margaret G. Burroughs, Editors. Detroit: Broadside Press, 1969, p. 70.

999. Jackson, Mae. "I Remember...," *Celebrations: A New Anthology of Black American Poetry*, Arnold Adoff, Editor. Chicago: Follett Publishing Co., 1977, p 183.

1000. Jones, LeRoi. "A Poem for Black Hearts," *For Malcolm X: Poems on the Life and Death of Malcolm X*, Dudley Randall and Margaret G. Burroughs, Editors. Detroit: Broadside Press, 1969, p. 61.

1001. Jones, LeRoi. "A Poem for Black Hearts," A Broadside Treasury, Gwendolyn Brooks, Editor. Detroit: Broadside Press, 1971, p. 28.

1002. Jones, Ted. "My Ace of Spades," For Malcolm X: Poems on the Life and Death of Malcolm X, Dudley Randall and Margaret G. Burroughs, Editors. Detroit: Broadside Press, 1969, p. 5.

1003. __________. "My Ace of Spades," A Broadside Treasury, Gwendolyn Brooks, Editor. Detroit: Broadside Press, 1971, p. 15.

1004. __________. "True Blues for a Dues Payer," For Malcolm X: Poems on the Life and Death of Malcolm X, Dudley Randall and Margaret G. Burroughs, Editors. Detroit: Broadside Press, 1969, p. 25.

1005. Johnson, Christine C. "My Brother Malcolm," For Malcolm X: Poems on the Life and Death of Malcolm X, Dudley Randall and Margaret G. Burroughs, Editors. Detroit: Broadside Press, 1969, p. 3.

1006. __________. "When You Died," For Malcolm X: Poems on the Life and Death of Malcolm X, Dudley Randall and Margaret G. Burroughs, Editors. Detroit: Broadside Press, 1969, p. 71.

1007. Kgositsile, K. William. "Brother Malcolm's Echo," For Malcolm X: Poems on the Life and Death of Malcolm X, Dudley Randall and Margaret G. Burroughs, Editors. Detroit: Broadside Press, 1969, p. 55.

1008. __________. "Brother Malcolm's Echo," A Broadside Treasury, Gwendolyn Brooks, Editor. Detroit: Broadside Press, 1971, p. 27.

1009. Knight, Etheridge. "For Malcolm, a Year After," For Malcolm X: Poems on the Life and Death of Malcolm X, Dudley Randall and Margaret G. Burroughs, Editors. Detroit: Broadside Press, 1969, p. 43.

1010. __________. "It Was A Funky Deal," For Malcolm X: Poems on the Life and Death of Malcolm X, Dudley Randall and Margaret G. Burroughs, Editors. Detroit: Broadside Press, 1969, p. 21.

1011. __________. "Portrait of Malcolm X," Celebrations: A New Anthology of Black American Poetry, Arnold Adoff, Editor. Chicago: Follett Publishing Co., 1977, p. 180.

1012. __________. "The Sun Came," For Malcolm X: Poems on the Life and Death of Malcolm X, Dudley Randall and Margaret G. Burroughs, Editors. Detroit: Broadside Press, 1969, p. 73.

1013. LaGrone. "No Tomb in Arlington," For Malcolm X: Poems on the Life and Death of Malcolm X, Dudley Randall and Margaret G. Burroughs, Editors. Detroit: Broadside Press, 1969, p. 74.

1014. Lawrence, Joyce Whitsitt. "For Malcolm," A Broadside Treasury, Gwendolyn Brooks, Editor. Detroit: Broadside Press, 1971, p. 23.

1015. Llorens, David. "One Year Ago," For Malcolm X: Poems on the Life and Death of Malcolm X, Dudley Randall and Margaret G. Burroughs, Editors. Detroit: Broadside Press, 1969, p. 19.

1016. Lucas, James R. "Caution," For Malcolm X: Poems on the Life and Death of Malcolm X, Dudley Randall and Margaret G. Burroughs, Editors. Detroit: Broadside Press, 1969, p. 11.

1017. Major, Clarence. "Brother Malcolm: Waste Limit," For Malcolm X: Poems on the Life and Death of Malcolm X, Dudley Randall and Margaret G. Burroughs, Editors. Detroit: Broadside Press, 1969, p. 8.

1018. ______________. "Death of the Man," For Malcolm X: Poems on the Life and Death of Malcolm X, Dudley Randall and Margaret G. Burroughs, Editors. Detroit: Broadside Press, 1969, p. 26.

1019. ______________. "They Feared That He Believed," For Malcolm X: Poems on the Life and Death of Malcolm X, Dudley Randall and Margaret G. Burroughs, Editors. Detroit: Broadside Press, 1969, p. 6.

1020. McLlnay, Patricia. "Two For Malcolm," Black Scholar, Vol. 6, No. 2, Spring, 1966, p. 135.

1021. Moses, Gil. "Simple Finally Speaks Out to White Liberal About Malcolm X," Liberator, Vol. 6, No. 3, March, 1966, p. 15.

1022. Mumia, B. P. P. "A Prayer to El Hajj Malik," The Black Panther, May 19, 1970, p. 18.

1023. Neal, Larry. "The Summer After Malcolm," Black Boogaloo. San Francisco, CA: Journal of Black Poetry Press, 1969, p. 34.

1024. __________. "Malcolm X-An Autobiography," Black Boogaloo. San Francisco, CA: Journal of Black Poetry Press, 1969, pp. 35-36.

1025. __________. "Morning Raga for Malcolm," Black Boogaloo. San Francisco, CA: Journal of Black Poetry Press, 1969, p. 37.

1026. __________. "Malcolm X-An Autobiography," *A Broadside Treasury*, Gwendolyn Brooks, Editor. Detroit: Broadside Press, 1971, pp. 17-18.

1027. __________. "Morning Raga for Malcolm," *A Broadside Treasury*, Gwendolyn Brooks, Editor. Detroit: Boradside Press, 1971, p. 19.

1028. Neal, Lawrence P. "Malcolm X-An Autobiography," *For Malcolm X: Poems on the Life and Death of Malcolm X*, Dudley Randall and Margaret G. Burroughs, Editors. Detroit: Broadside Press, 1969, p. 9.

1029. ______________. "Morning Raga for Malcolm," *For Malcolm X: Poems on the Life and Death of Malcolm X*, Dudley Randall and Margaret G. Burroughs, Editors. Detroit: Broadside Press, 1969, p. 19.

1030. "Ode to Malcolm X," *Black Power Speaks* (Published by the Universal Coloured Peoples Association of London), June, 1968.

1031. Patricia. "Two for Malcolm," *For Malcolm X: Poems on the Life and Death of Malcolm X*, Dudley Randall and Margaret G. Burroughs, Editors. Detroit: Broadside Press, 1969, p. 31.

1032. Patterson, Raymond. "At That Moment," *For Malcolm X: Poems on the Life and Death of Malcolm X*, Dudley Randall and Margaret G. Burroughs, Editors. Detroit: Broadside Press, 1969, p. 69.

1033. ________________. "At That Moment," *A Broadside Treasury*, Gwendolyn Brooks, Editor. Detroit: Broadside Press, 1971, p. 29.

1034. ________________. "Ballada o Neizvestnosti," *For Malcolm X: Poems on the Life and Death of Malcolm X*, Dudley Randall and Margaret G. Burroughs, Editors. Detroit: Broadside Press, 1969, p. 76.

1035. ________________. "Ballad to the Anonymous," *For Malcolm X: Poems on the Life and Death of Malcolm X*, Dudley Randall and Margaret G. Burroughs, Editors. Detroit: Broadside Press, 1969, p. 77.

1036. Qeigless, Helen. "Days After," *For Malcolm X: Poems on the Life and Death of Malcolm X*, Dudley Randall and Margaret G. Burroughs, Editors. Detroit: Broadside Press, 1969, p. 65.

1037. Richer, Edward. "Some Whites Mourn Malcolm, As If," *For Malcolm X: Poems on the Life and Death of Malcolm X*, Dudley Randall and Margaret G. Burroughs, Editors. Detroit: Broadside Press, 1969, p. 37.

1038. Rivers, Conrad Kent. "If Blood Is Black Then Spirit Neglects My Unborn Son," *For Malcolm X: Poems on the Life and Death of Malcolm X*, Dudley Randall and Margaret G. Burroughs, Editors. Detroit: Broadside Press, 1969, p. 27.

1039. ____________________. "If Blood Is Black Then Spirit Neglects My Unborn Son," *A Broadside Treasury*, Gwendolyn Brooks, Editor. Detroit: Broadside Press, 1971, p. 24.

1040. ____________________. "Look Homeward, Malcolm," *For Malcolm X: Poems on the Life and Death of Malcolm X*, Dudley Randall and Margaret G. Burroughs, Editors. Detroit: Broadside Press, 1969, p. 66.

1041. ____________________. "Malcolm, A Thousandth Poem," *Celebrations: A New Anthology of Black American Poetry*, Arnold Adoff, Editor. Chicago: Follett Publishing Co., 1977, p. 183.

1042. Russell, Carlos Enrique. "For Malcolm X," *Liberator*, Vol. 5, No. 4, April, 1965, p. 8.

1043. Sanchez, Sonia. "Malcolm," *For Malcolm X: Poems on the Life and Death of Malcolm X*, Dudley Randall and Margaret G. Burroughs, Editors. Detroit: Broadside Press, 1969, p. 88.

1044. _______________. "Malcolm," *A Broadside Treasury*, Gwendolyn Brooks, Editor. Detroit: Broadside Press, 1971, p. 25.

1045. Sinclair, John. "The Destruction of America," *For Malcolm X: Poems on the Life and Death of Malcolm X*, Dudley Randall and Margaret G. Burroughs, Editors. Detroit: Broadside Press, 1969, p. 58.

1046. Snellings, Roland. "Earth (for Mrs. Mary Bethune and the African and Afro-American Woman)," *Soulbook 2*, Vol. 1, No. 2, Spring, 1965, pp. 131-132.

1047. Spriggs, Edward S. "Berkeley's Blue Black," *For Malcolm X: Poems on the Life and Death of Malcolm X*, Dudley Randall and Margaret G. Burroughs, Editors. Detroit: Broadside Press, 1969, p. 74.

1048. __________________. "For Brother Malcolm," *For Malcolm X: Poems on the Life and Death of Malcolm X*, Dudley Randall and Margaret G. Burroughs, Editors. Detroit: Broadside Press, 1969, p. 73.

1049. __________________. "For Brother Malcolm," *A Broadside Treasury*, Gwendolyn Brooks, Editor. Detroit: Broadside Press, 1971, p. 30.

1050. _________________. "Stillborn Pollen Falling," For Malcolm X: Poems on the Life and Death of Malcolm X, Dudley Randall AND Margaret G. Burroughs, Editors. Detroit: Broadside Press, 1969, p. 72.

1051. Thompson, Julius. "To Malcolm X," My Black Me: A Beginning Book of Black Poetry, Arnold Adoff, Editor. New York: E. P. Dutton & Co., 1974, p. 57.

1052. Troupe, Quincy. "For Malcolm Who Walks in the Eyes of Our Children," Celebrations: A New Anthology of Black American Poetry, Arnold Adoff, Editor. Chicago: Follett Publishing Co., 1977, p. 187.

1053. Walker, Margaret. "For Malcolm," For Malcolm X: Poems on the Life and Death of Malcolm X, Dudley Randall and Margaret G. Burroughs, Editors. Detroit: Broadside Press, 1969, p. 32.

1054. _________________. "For Malcolm X," Celebrations: A New Anthology of Black American Poetry, Arnold Adoff, Editor. Chicago: Follett Publishing Co., 1977, p. 181-182.

1055. Watkins, Mel, Editor. "Malcolm X's Birthday", Black Review, No. 2. New York: William Morrow & Co., 1972, p. 77.

1056. Whitsitt, Joyce. "For Malcolm," For Malcolm X: Poems on the Life and Death of Malcolm X, Dudley Randall and Margaret G. Burroughs, Editors. Detroit: Broadside Press, 1969, p. 20.

1057. Wilson, August. "For Malcolm X and Others," Negro Digest, Vol. 18, No. 11, September, 1969, p. 58.

1058. Wilson, Reginald. "For Our American Cousins," For Malcolm X: Poems on the Life and Death of Malcolm X, Dudley Randall and Margaret G. Burroughs, Editors. Detroit: Broadside Press, 1969, p. 35.

1059. Worley, James. "Color Schema," For Malcolm X: Poems on the Life and Death of Malcolm X, Dudley Randall and Margaret G. Burroughs, Editors. Detroit: Broadside Press, 1969, p. 65.

1060. _______________. "De Gustibus," For Malcolm X: Poems on the Life and Death of Malcolm X, Dudley Randall and Margaret G. Burroughs, Editors. Detroit: Broadside Press, 1969, p. 26.

1061. _______________. "Let 'X' Be Hope," For Malcolm X: Poems on the Life and Death of Malcolm X, Dudley Randall and Margaret G. Burroughs, Editors. Detroit: Broadside Press, 1969, p. 68.

1062. _____________. "Sleep Bitter, Brother," For Malcolm X: Poems on the Life and Death of Malcolm X, Dudley Randall and Margaret G. Burroughs, Editors. Detroit: Broadside Press, 1969, p. 23.

1063. _____________. "The Cost," For Malcolm X: Poems on the Life and Death of Malcolm X, Dudley Randall and Margaret G. Burroughs, Editors. Detroit: Broadside Press, 1969, p. 5.

1064. Wright, Jay. "The Solitude of Change," For Malcolm X: Poems on the Life and Death of Malcolm X, Dudley Randall and Margaret G. Burroughs, Editors. Detroit: Broadside Press, 1969, p. 28.

1065. Wright, Julia. "To Malcolm X," Presence Africaine, Second Quarter, 1965, p. 239 (French Edition).

D
Book Reviews

A Selected List

1. THE AUTOBIOGRAPHY OF MALCOLM X

1066. Adair, Anthony. The Autobiography of Malcolm X, by Malcolm X, Contemporary Review, Vol. 209, No. 1206, July, 1966, pp. 49-50.

1067. The Autobiography of Malcolm X, by Malcolm X, Booklist, Vol. 62, January 1, 1966, p. 423.

1068. The Autobiography of Malcolm X, by Malcolm X, Choice, Vol. 2, January, 1966, p. 764.

1069. The Autobiography of Malcolm X, by Malcolm X, Choice, Vol. 16, December, 1969, p. 1274.

1070. The Autobiography of Malcolm X, by Malcolm X, Christian Science Monitor, Vol. 57, December 2, 1965, p. 84.

1071. The Autobiography of Malcolm X, by Malcolm X, Economist, Vol. 219, June 18, 1966, p. 1319.

1072. The Autobiography of Malcolm X, New Yorker, Vol. 43, No. 39, November 13, 1965, pp. 246-247.

1073. The Autobiography of Malcolm X, by Malcolm X, Saturday Review, Vol. 49, July 3, 1966, p. 39.

1074. The Autobiography of Malcolm X, The Speeches of Malcolm at Harvard, and Malcolm X, The Man and His Times, Time, Vol. 95, No. 8, February 23, 1970, pp. 88-90.

1075. The Autobiography of Malcolm X, by Malcolm X, Times Literary Supplement, June 9, 1966, p. 39.

1076. Bone, R. The Autobiography of Malcolm X, by Malcolm X, New York Times Book Review, Vol. 7, September 11, 1966, p. 3.

1077. Breitman, George. The Autobiography of Malcolm X, The Militant, October 18, 1965, p. 4.

1078. Capouya, Emile. "A Brief Return From Mecca: The Autobiography of Malcolm X," Saturday Review, Vol. 48, No. 47, November 20, 1965, pp. 42-43.

1079. Chevigny, Bell Gale. "Malcolm X's Autobiography," Village Voice, March 3, 1966.

1080. Clarke, John Henrik. The Autobiography of Malcolm X, by Malcolm X, Black Scholar, Vol. 6, No. 1, Winter, 1966, pp. 48-52.

1081. Hentoff, Nathan. The Autobiography of Malcolm X, by Malcolm X, Commonweal, Vol. 83, January 28, 1966, p. 511.

1082. Holt, Len. The Autobiography of Malcolm X, Liberator, Vol. 6, No. 2, February, 1966, pp. 22-23.

1083. Jackson, Miles M. Jr. The Autobiography of Malcolm X, by Malcolm X, Library Journal, Vol. 91, No. 1, January 1, 1966, p. 101.

1084. Kretz, Thomas. "Journey Toward Truth," Christian Century, Vol. 82, No. 99, December 8, 1965, p. 1513. Book review of The Autobiography of Malcolm X, by Malcolm X.

1085. MacGregor, Martha. The Autobiography of Malcolm X, New York Post, November 14, 1965.

1086. MacInness, C. The Autobiography of Malcolm X, by Malcolm X, Spectator, May 27, 1966, p. 668.

1087. Morrison, Derrick. The Autobiography of Malcolm X, Young Socialist, Vol. 9, No. 2, November-December, 1965, pp. 20-21.

1088. Nelson, Truman. "Delinquent's Progress," Nation, Vol. 201, No. 15, November 8, 1965, pp. 336, 337, 338. Book review of The Autobiography of Malcolm X, by Malcolm X.

1089. Rustin, Bayard. The Autobiography of Malcolm X, The Washington Post, November 14, 1965, pp. 1, 8-10, 16, 17.

1090. Samuels, Gertrude. "Satan in the Ghetto," Newsweek, Vol. 66, November 15, 1965, pp. 130-132. A review of The Autobiography of Malcolm X, by Malcolm X.

1091. Short, C. The Autobiography of Malcolm X, by Malcolm X, Punch, Vol. 250, June 22, 1966, p. 924.

1092. Small, Richard. The Autobiography of Malcolm X, by Malcolm X, Race, Vol. 8, No. 2, October, 1966, pp. 190-191.

1093. Stone, I. J. "The Pilgrimage of Malcolm X," New York Review, November 11, 1965. Review of two books: The Autobiography of Malcolm X, by Malcolm X, and Malcolm X Speaks, edited by George Breitman.

1094. Thorpe, Earl E. The Autobiography of Malcolm X, by Malcolm X, Social Education, Vol. 33, No. 4, April, 1969, pp. 489-491.

1095. Toynbee, P. The Autobiography of Malcolm X, by Malcolm X, Observer, May 22, 1966, p. 26.

1096. Weatherbuy, W. J. The Autobiography of Malcolm X, by Malcolm X, Manchester Guardian, Vol. 94, June 9, 1966, p. 10.

1097. Weiss, Samuel. The Autobiography of Malcolm X, by Malcolm X, Chicago Jewish Forum, Vol. 25, No. 24, Summer, 1967, pp. 305-306.

2. MALCOLM X SPEAKS

1098. Brogan, H. Malcolm X Speaks, George Breitman, Editor, Manchester Guardian, Vol. 95, August 25, 1966, p. 10.

1099. Daniel, Jack L. Malcolm X Speaks, George Breitman, Editor, Speech Teacher, Vol. 19, March, 1970, pp. 146-147.

1100. Holt, Len. Malcolm X Speaks, George Breitman, Editor, Liberator, Vol. 5, No. 2, February, 1966, p. 22.

1101. Llorens, D. Malcolm X Speaks, George Breitman, Editor, Negro Digest, Vol. 15, May, 1966, p. 89.

1102. Malcolm X Speaks, George Breitman, Editor, Booklist, Vol. 62, February 1, 1966, p. 506.

1103. Malcolm X Speaks, George Breitman, Editor, Choice, Vol. 3, June, 1966, p. 297.

1104. Morrison, Derrick. Malcolm X Speaks, George Breitman, Editor, Young Socialist, Vol. 9, No. 2, November-December, 1965, pp. 21-22.

1105. Sheppard, Barry. Malcolm X Speaks, George Breitman, Editor, The Militant, December 5, 1966, p. 4.

3. FOR MALCOLM X: POEMS ON THE LIFE AND DEATH OF MALCOLM X

1106. Saunders, George. For Malcolm: Poems on the Life and Death of Malcolm X, The Militant, September 4, 1967, p. 9.

4. THE LAST YEARS OF MALCOLM X: THE EVOLUTION OF A REVOLUTIONARY

1107. The Last Years of Malcolm X: The Evolution of a Revolutionary, Choice, December, 1967, p. 1170.

5. THE SPEECHES OF MALCOLM X AT HARVARD

1108. Jefferson, Pat. The Speeches of Malcolm X at Harvard, Edited by Archie Epps, Quarterly Journal of Speech, Vol. 54, No. 3, October, 1968, p. 314.

6. MALCOLM X: THE MAN AND HIS TIMES

1109. Hamilton, Charles V. Malcolm X: The Man and His Times, John Henrik Clarke, Editor, New York Book Review, September 28, 1969, pp. 3, 51.

1110. Hamilton, William. Malcolm X: The Man and His Times, John Henrik Clarke, Editor, Christian Century, Vol. 87, February 11, 1970, p. 177.

1111. Malcolm X: The Man and His Times, John Henrik Clarke, Editor, Time, Vol. 95, February 23, 1970, p. 88.

1112. Malcolm X: The Man and His Times, John Henrik Clarke, Editor, Choice, Vol. 7, June, 1970, p. 583.

1113. Malcolm X: The Man and His Times, John Henrik Clarke, Editor, Virginia Quarterly Review, Vol. 46, Spring, 1970, p. lxx.

1114. Osnos, Peter. Malcolm X: The Man and His Times, John Henrik Clarke, Editor, Washington Post, November 10, 1969, Leisure Section, p. D-8.

1115. Storey, Elizabeth. Malcolm X: The Man and His Times, John Henrik Clarke, Editor, Library Journal, Vol. 95, No. 6, March 15, 1970, p. 1212.

7. MALCOLM X: BY ANY MEANS NECESSARY

1116. Blackwell, Angela. Malcolm X: By Any Means Necessary: Speeches, Interviews and A Letter by Malcolm X, George Breitman, Editor, Black Scholar, Vol. 1, No. 7, May, 1970, pp. 56-57.

1117. Morrison, Derrick. Malcolm X: By Any Means Necessary, George Breitman, Editor, The Militant, April 3, 1970, p. 15.

1118. Smith, Lee. Malcolm X: By Any Means Necessary, George Breitman, Editor, International Socialist Review, May, 1970.

8. THE DEATH AND LIFE OF MALCOLM X

1119. Breitman, George. The Death and Life of Malcolm X, by Peter Goldman, The Militant, March 9, 1973.

1120. Coombs, Orde. The Death and Life of Malcolm X, by Peter Goldman, New York Times Book Review, January 28, 1973, p. 40.

1121. Lowe, Walter J. The Death and Life of Malcolm X, by Peter Goldman, The Newark Sunday Star Ledger, February 11, 1973.

1122. The Death and Life of Malcolm X, by Peter Goldman, Freedomways, Second Quarter, 1973, pp. 160-162.

9. THE ASSASSINATION OF MALCOLM X

1123. The Assassination of Malcolm X, by George Breitman, et al, Encore, July 5, 1977, p. 48.

E
Audio-Visual Materials

A Selected List

1. WORKS BY MALCOLM X

1124. "Harlem 'Hate-gang' Scare." Militant Labor Forum. May 29, 1964. Part V (Audiotape). New York, 1964. No. 1 on sides 1 and 2 of tape cassette.

1125. "The African Revolution and its Effect on the Afro-American. Haryou Act rally. Dec. 12, 1964." Part II (Audiotape). New York, 1964. No. 1 on side 1 of tape cassette. Duration of program: 28' 30". Question and answer period following Malcolm X's speech. Part of the Schomburg Center Oral History Tape Collection.

1126. "The African Revolution and its Impact on the American Negro. Harvard Law School forum. Dec. 16, 1964." Part I (Audiotape). Cambridge, MA, 1964. No. 1 on sides 1 and 2 of tape cassette. Duration of speech: 50' 38". Malcolm X discusses the situation in America with respect to Blacks, and Black nationalism and contemporary African affairs. Transcript of speech contained in X, Malcolm. The speeches of Malcolm X at Harvard, pp. 161-182. Classmark: 323.173-X. Part of the Schomburg Center Oral History Tape Collection.

1127. "The African Revolution and its Effect on the Afro-American. Haryou Act rally. Dec. 12, 1964." Part I (Audiotape). New York, 1964. No. 1 on sides 1 and 2 of tape cassette. Black author. Duration of speech: 55' 00". Malcolm X discusses Black nationalism, the new Black self-image being created in Africa, the American civil rights movement, and media-created images. Excerpts from speech contained in: X Malcolm. Malcolm X speaks, pp. 229-230; 232-235. Classmark: Sc 323.173-X. Part of the Schomburg Center Oral History Tape Collection.

1128. "Prospects for Freedom in 1965. Militant Labor Forum. Jan. 7, 1965." Part I (Audiotape). New York, 1965. No. 1 on sides 1 and 2 of tape cassette. Black author. Duration of speech: 71' 08". Forum held at the Palm Gardens in New York City. Malcolm X discusses Black militancy and the civil rights movement, Black nationalism, contemporary African political trends, the Black Muslim movement, and media-created images. Excerpted transcript of speech contained in: X, Malcolm. Malcolm X Speaks, pp. 160-170, 212, 215, 216-217, 221-226, 227-228, 238-240, 245. Classmark: Sc 323.173-X. Part of the Schomburg Center Oral History Tape Collection.

1129. "Prospects for Freedom in 1965. Militant Labor Forum, Jan. 7, 1965." Part II (Audiotape). New York, 1965. No. 1 on side 1 of tape cassette. Duration of program: 40' 12". Forum held at the Palm Gardens in New York City. Question and answer session following Malcolm X's speech. Conclusion of the question and answer session not recorded. Part of the Schomburg Center Oral History Tape Collection.

1130. "Young Socialist Interview with Malcolm X. Jan. 18, 1965." (Audiotape). New York, 1965. No. 1 on side 2 of tape cassette. Black author. Duration of program: 35' 34". Malcolm X interviewed by Barry Sheppard and Jack Barnes of the Young Socialist Alliance. Malcolm X discusses his definition of Black nationalism. Transcript of interview contained in: X, Malcolm. By Any Means Necessary, pp. 157-166. Classmark: Sc 323.173-X. Part of the Schomburg Center Oral History Tape Collection.

1131. "Malcolm X on Afro-American History. Jan. 24, 1965." Part I (Audiotape). New York, 1965. On 2 cassettes. Duration of speech: 100' 29". Speech of Malcolm X to the Organization of Afro-American Unity. Malcolm X discusses African history and the Afro-American's historical roots. Transcript of speech contained in: X, Malcolm. Malcolm X on Afro-American History, pp. 3-48. Classmark: Sc 973-X. Part of the Schomburg Center Oral History Collection.

1132. "Malcolm X on Afro-American History. Jan. 24, 1965." Part II (Audiotape). New York, 1965. No. 1 on side 1 of tape cassette. Black author. Duration of speech: 27' 25". Speech of Malcolm X to the Organization of Afro-American Unity. Question and answer period following Malcolm X's speech. Part of the Schomburg Center Oral History Tape Collection.

1133. "Interview with Malcolm X and Harry Ring of WBAI. Jan. 28, 1965." (Audiotape). New York, 1965. No. 2 on side 1 of tape cassette. Duration of speech: 15' 02". WBAI-FM interview with Malcolm X. Malcolm X discusses his political and religious philosophy subsequent to his break with the Black Muslims, and United States foreign policy in Africa and Asia. Excerpted transcripts of interview contained in: X, Malcolm. Malcolm X Speaks, pp. 217, 237, 242-244. Classmark: Sc 323.173-X. Part of the Schomburg Center Oral History Tape Collection.

1134. "Interview with Malcolm X at The London School of Economics. Feb. 1965." (Audiotape). London, 1965. No. 1 on side 1 of tape cassette. Duration of speech: 35' 05". Malcolm X discusses racism in America, U. S. foreign policy and Black nationalism. Also discussed are contemporary African struggles for independence. Part of the Schomburg Center Oral History Tape Collection.

1135. "The Crisis of Racism. Palm Gardens, New York City. May 1, 1962." Part III (Audiotape). New York, 1962. No. 2 on side 2 of tape cassette.

1136. "The Crisis of Racism. Palm Gardens, New York City, May 1, 1962." Part IV (Audiotape). New York, 1962. No. 1 on sides 1 and 2 of tape.

1137. "Speech of Malcolm X at CCNY. Nov. 7, 1963." (Audiotape). New York, 1963. On 2 cassettes. Black author. Duration of speech: 95' 18". Speech of Malcolm X at the City College of New York. Malcolm X outlines the philosophy of the Black Muslims, speaking as a representative of Elijah Muhammed. Part of the Schomburg Center Oral History Tape Collection.

1138. "The Ballot or the Bullet." Cleveland. (Audiotape). Cleveland, 1964. No. 1 on side 1 and 2 of tape cassette.

1139. "The Battle or the Bullet." Detroit. (Audiotape). Detroit, 1964. No. 1 on sides 1 and 2 of tape cassette.

1140. "Harlem 'Hate-gang' Scare. Militant Labor Forum. May 29, 1964." Part IV (Audiotape). New York, 1964. No. 1 on side 2 of tape cassette.

1141. "The Black Revolution. Militant Labor Forum. Palm Gardens, New York City. April 8, 1964." Part I (Audiotape). New York, 1964. No. 1 on side 1 of tape cassette. Black author. Duration of speech: 46' 15". Speech of Malcolm X at the Militant Labor Forum held at Palm Gardens in New York City. Malcolm X discusses Black nationalism. Transcript of speech contained in: X, Malcolm. Malcolm X Speaks, pp. 48-62. Classmark: Sc 323.173-X. Part of the Schomburg Center Oral History Tape Collection.

1142. "The Black Revolution. Militant Labor Forum. Palm Gardens, New York City. April 8, 1964." Part II (Audiotape). New York, 1964. No. 1 on side 2 of tape cassette. Black author. Duration of program: 41' 47". Speech of Malcolm X at the Militant Labor Forum held at Palm Gardens in New York City. Question and answer period following Malcolm X's speech. Transcript of speech contained in: X, Malcolm. Malcolm X Speaks, pp. 48-62. Classmark: Sc 323-173-X. Part of the Schomburg Center Oral History Tape Collection.

1143. "The Ballot or the Bullet. Cleveland." (Audiotape). Cleveland, 1964. No. 1 on side 1 and 2 of tape cassette. Duration of speech: 77' 20". Malcolm X's speech, The Ballot or the Bullet, given on April 3, 1964 at the Cory Mehtodist Church at a meeting sponsored by the Cleveland chapter of the Congress of Racial Equality. In this speech, Malcolm X outlines his philosophy of Black nationalism subsequent to his break with the Black Muslims and his founding of the Muslim Mosque, Inc. This speech, given at a symposium entitled The Negro Revolt - What Comes Next?, follows the speech of Louis E. Lomax of Cleveland CORE. This speech is one of two by Malcolm X entitled The Ballot or the Bullet in the Schomburg Center for Research in Black Culture of The New York Public Library. Transcript of the Cleveland version contained in: X, Malcolm. Malcolm X Speaks, pp. 23-47. Classmark: Sc 323.173-X. Part of the Schomburg Center Oral History Tape Collection.

1144. "The Ballot or the Bullet. Detroit." (Audiotape). Detroit, 1964. No. 1 on sides 1 and 2 of tape cassette. Duration of speech: 54' 28" Malcolm X's speech, The Ballot or the Bullet, given in Detroit. In this speech Malcolm X outlines his philosophy of Black nationalism subsequent to his break with the Black Muslims and his founding of the Muslim Mosque, Inc. This speech is one of two by Malcolm X entitled The Ballot or the Bullet in the Schomburg Center for Research in Black Culture of the New York Public Library. The Detroit version was originally released as a record album under the title: Ballots or Bullets, released by First Amendment Records (LP-FAR 100) and distributed by the Jamie/Guyden Distributing Corp. of Philadelphia. Malcolm X's Detroit version of The Ballot or the Bullet was recorded by Milton R. Henry. Part of the Schomburg Center Oral History Tape Collection.

2. <u>WORKS ABOUT MALCOLM X</u>

1145. "Malcolm X memorial. April, 1965." Part I (Audiotape). New York? 1965. No. 1 on side 1 of tape cassette.

1146. "Malcolm X memorial. April, 1965." Part II (Audiotape). New York? 1965. No. 1 on sides 1 and 2 of tape cassette.

1147. "Malcolm X Memorial. April, 1965." Part III (Audiotape). New York? 1965. No. 1 on sides 1 and 2 of tape cassette.

1148. Breitman, George. "The Legacy of Malcolm X." Part I (Audiotape). New York? 1966? No. 1 on sides 1 and 2 of tape cassette.

1149. ________________. "The Legacy of Malcolm X." Part II (Audiotape). New York? 1966? No. 1 on sides 1 and 2 of tape cassette.

1150. ________________. "The Legacy of Malcolm X." Part III (Audiotape). New York? 1966? No. 1 on sides 1 and 2 of tape cassette.

1151. ________________. "The Legacy of Malcolm X." Part IV (Audiotape). New York? 1966? No. 1 on sides 1 and 2 of tape cassette.

1152. ________________. "The Political Development of Malcolm X." (Audiotape). New York? 1966? No. 1 on side 2 of tape cassette.

1153. ________________. "The Wit and Wisdom of Malcolm X." (Audiotape). New York? 1966? No. 1 on sides 1 and 2 of tape cassette.

1154. Norden, Eric. "The CIA and its Role in Malcolm X's Assassination." Detroit Militant Labor Forum. March 11, 1966 (Audiotape). Detroit, 1966. No. 1 on side 1 of tape cassette.

1155. Porter, Herman. "The Trial and the Role of the Police in the Malcolm X Assassination." Part I. Detroit Militant Labor Forum. March 11, 1965 (Audiotape). Detroit, 1965. No. 1 on side 1 and 2 of tape cassette.

1156. ______________. "The Trial and the Role of the Police in the Malcolm X Assassination." Part II. Detroit Militant Labor Forum. March 11, 1965 (Audiotape). Detroit, 1965. No. 1 on side 1 of tape cassette.

1157. "Socialist Workers' Party Symposium in Memory of Malcolm X. February, 1966." Part I (Audiotape). New York? 1966. Nol 1 on side 1 of tape cassette.

1158. "Socialist Workers' Party Symposium in Memory of Malcolm X. February, 1966." Part II (Audiotape). New York? 1966. No. 1 on side 2 of tape cassette.

1159. "Socialist Workers' Party Symposium in Memory of Malcolm X. February, 1966." Part III (Audiotape.) New York? 1966. No. 2 on side 2 of tape cassette.

1160. "Socialist Workers' Party Symposium in Memory of Malcolm X. February, 1966." Part IV (Audiotape). New York? 1966. No. 1 on side 1 of tape cassette.

F
Records

A Selected List

1. Malcolm X. Ballots or Bullets. First Amendment Records LP-FAR 100
2. _________. The Last Message. (2 records) Discos Hablando LP 1300-1301
3. _________. Malcolm X: Excerpts and Music from the Sound Track. (Phonodisc) Warner Bros. Records BS2619
4. _________. Malcolm X: His Wit and Wisdom. Douglas Records Co.
5. _________. Malcolm X Speaking. Ethnic Records E-1265
6. _________. Malcolm Speaks Again. 20 Grand LP-100
7. _________. Malcolm X Talks to Young People. Douglas International Corp. SD 795
8. _________. Message to the Grass Roots from Malcolm X. Afro Records AA-1264

G
Namesakes, Screenplay, and Broadside

A Selected List

1. NAMESAKES

1. "Malcolm X Association"
   Located on various college campuses

2. "Malcolm X College"
   Chicago, Illinois

3. "Malcolm X Day"
   Celebrated in various cities throughout the United States

4. "Malcolm X Festival"
   Philadelphia, Pennsylvania

5. "Malcolm X Liberation University"
   Durham, North Carolina
   Founded in 1969

6. "Malcolm X Montessori School"
   Oakland, California

7. "Malcolm X Mosque"
   Harlem, New York

8. "Malcolm X Organization of Afro-American Unity, Inc."

9. "Malcolm X Park" (Meridian Hill Park)
   Washington, D.C.

10. "Malcolm X Scholarship Fund"
    Established at various colleges in the United States

11. "Malcolm X Square"
    Boston, Massachusetts

2. SCREENPLAY

1. Baldwin, James. _One Day, When I Was Lost: A Scenario Based on Alex Haley's "The Autobiography of Malcolm X._ New York: Dail Press, 1973. 280 pp.

   This is a screenplay based on _The Autobiography of Malcolm X_.

3. BROADSIDE

1. Howard University Department of Drama Presents "El Hajj Malik: A Play About Malcolm X," by N. R. Davidson, Jr., October 9-14, 1980, 8:00 p.m. Broadside.

H
Documentaries and Filmstrip

A Selected List

1. DOCUMENTARIES

1. "Malcolm X: Struggle for Freedom" (1964)
   Documentary 16 mm, 22 minutes

2. "The Significance of Malcolm X" (1969)
   Documentary 16 mm, 30 minutes

3. "Tribute to Malcolm X" (1969)
   16 mm

4. "Protest: Black Power" (1969)
   16 mm sound and color, 15 minutes
   Excerpts from interviews and speeches, including Malcolm X.

5. "Malcolm X" (1970)
   Documentary 16 mm, 23 minutes

6. "Malcolm X Speaks" (1971)
   Documentary 16 mm, 55 minutes

7. "Malcolm X" (1972)
   Documentary 16 mm, 92 minutes

2. FILMSTRIP

1. "The Search for Black Identity: Malcolm X" (Filmstrip). Pleasantville, NY. Guidance Associates, 1970. 34 minutes

Index

Including authors, joint authors, and editors.
Numbers refer to individual entry numbers.

ABOUT THE COMPILER

LENWOOD G. DAVIS is Associate Professor of History at Winston-Salem State University. He received both his B.A. and M.A. degrees in history from North Carolina Central University, Durham, North Carolina, and a doctorate in history from Carnegie-Mellon University. Dr. Davis has compiled more than seventy bibliographies. He is the author of ten books, *I Have a Dream: The Life and Times of Martin Luther King, Jr.* (1973), *The Black Woman in American Society: A Selected Annotated Bibliography* (1975), *The Black Family in the United States: A Selected Bibliography of Annotated Books, Articles, and Dissertations on Black Families in America* (1978), *Sickle Cell Anemia: A Selected Annotated Bibliography* (1978), *Black Artists in the United States: An Annotated Bibliography*, coauthored with Janet L. Sims (1980), *Marcus Garvey: An Annotated Bibliography*, coauthored with Janet L. Sims (1980), *Black Aged in the United States* (1980), *Black Athletes in the United States: A Bibliography*, coauthored with Belinda S. Daniels (1981), *A Paul Robeson Research Guide* (1982), and *Joe Louis: A Selected Bibliography* (1983).